1

LLC-3, inc.
Arts Publishing
P.O. Box 23035, Ft.Lauderdale, FL 33307
Copyright 2007
All Rights Reserved
Printed in the United Sates of America

ISBN 978-1-4196-8358-9
1-4196-8358-6

Introduction:

As that famous yachtsman once said: was it Ted Turner, or Captain Queeg? "Humor is what happens to the other guy."One thing I learned early, boating can be hilarious! Sometimes a scream! Every boater I've known has tales of crazy things that happened "that day." How they got into, or out of a sticky situation, saved themselves from ultimate disaster. And threw great parties.

Starting with boats on the Ohio River, in Indiana, I owned a 'shipload' of water toys, from wooden river john boats to sailing prams, fishing boats, runabouts, ski terrors.

There was always a great story about "that day," the boat, weather, quirk of the moment, the people. Boating was our weekend cookout fun, our party mode, our ultimate escape from reality.

When I finally graduated to a boat big enough to live on, I found "that day" came more often. I had moved to Miami, then to Key Largo;earned a Captain's, then a Master's license, did some charters, delivered yachts to New York, St.Thomas, as far as Trinidad, the Amazon; lived on a succession of sails and trawlers, to 50 ft., and met wonderful people. I keep them all in fond memory, knowing we'll meet again some day, in some foreign port:

Say, aren't you...?

A short Bio of the Author

Capt. Chuck Gnaegy is a man obsessed by the sea; to be near it, in it, or on it. Grandson of a Mississippi River Boat Captain out of St. Louis, and Chester, Illinois – who held an 1875 patent for invention of a boat propeller – he recalls as a little boy, sitting on a dirt floor at his grand-father's place, waiting for the mud to settle in a glass of river water. "Tasted just like the river smelled, wild and free. I was hooked."

His first boat, a 10-foot wooden john boat he and boyhood friend Flavius Bradford found adrift, on the Ohio. The old water-logged boat needed constant bailing as they paddled the river – about a mile wide. It sank at a small island in the middle and they had to swim it back to shore.

Skipping school and skinny dipping, they got sunburns of their lives. His father didn't approve.

Later, he'd fish and ski at Kentucky Lake; catch a 25-lb. catfish on rod/reel. As his family grew, in Miami, his first ocean boat at Coconut Grove Sailing Club was Scorpio, 24-foot sloop. Then bigger and better: children grown, Key Largo on his 43-foot *My Word,* a motorsailer. He received a charter captain's ticket in 1979, later a master's license. He has delivered yachts from Miami to New York, St. Thomas, sailed south as far as Trinidad; swam in the Amazon, had many fishing and diving adventures in the Caribbean and Pacific as well. Read those adventures here.

A nationally acclaimed professional writer, photographer and artist, Capt. Chuck contributes to the major boating and adventure magazines, YachtForums.com, Yachts International, Powerboat Canada, Dockside, Motorboating, Sea, Yachting, Salt Water Sportsman, Sports Afield, Field & Stream, True, Argosy, Saga, Rudder, plus many major newspaper Sunday Travel Sections.

Served as Senior Editor of a Florida Boating Magazine and Marine Journal for several years, and now, from his base in South Florida, He specializes in travel and media reviews of large yachts -- 45 to 220 feet -- celebrity palaces.

############

"I hope you enjoy reading this as much as I have enjoyed living the good times; hilarious fun of being part of the yachtie world. It really is "A thousand miles from reality." I know tomorrow, next week, next month, "that day" will happen again. I can't wait."

Adventure Index

Dedicated to my two movie-star lovely cum-laude graduates, talented, intelligent daughters, Laurette & Leslie; namesakes Art & Mick Gnaegy; also my great partners and cohorts in these adventures; Capt. Carroll Kern, Frank Murphy, Dick Moore, Barbara Baker, Linda Cantrell, Tim Banse.

Pirates, Pearls & Paradise

Tales of the Caribbean South Seas & More

Entertaining, Exuberant, Sea Going "True Lies"

Capt. Chuck Gnaegy

A Creation of LLC-3 Arts Publishing
P.O. Box 23035, Ft. Lauderdale, FL 33307

*This
is a book of
short stories concocted
by the author, based on his own
experiences. All names and characters
are fictitious; any resemblance or
relationship to actual people,
places, or occurrences
is completely
coincidental*

©

One

Pirates in Caribbean History

The first peoples here were brown-skinned natives, Caribs. When Columbus sailed across the Atlantic, the first European to find these islands, he landed at Grand Turk, part of the Bahama chain. Thinking he had found the route to Asia, the East Indies; he named the people Indians. First of a wide assortment of rogues who came to settle and conquer, he was followed by Explorers, Religious Dissenters, Freebooters, Slaves, and Buccaneers, who eventually built great nations. The string of islands, just off the coast of Florida, to Trinidad – the West Indies – became known as the Caribbean, after the Carib Indians, though the Caribbean Sea starts at Haiti and the Dominican Republic. 100 years later the islands became havens for Pirates, who started as Privateers blessed by Governments but soon kept the booty for themselves. They headquartered at Port Royal, Jamaica, then Nassau, the Bahamas. Some lurked at Far Tortuga; they ravaged the Gulf of Mexico, New Orleans, Nevis, Caicos, Antigua, Guadalupe, Antigua, Barbados, Trinidad, Tobago. Pirate profiles start every chapter of this work, to introduce modern actions which coincide with the ancient even today, four to five centuries later.

Here's the first...

The Custody Caper
Privateers: A How-to of Modern, if not Illegal, Piracy

I crouched in the shadows next to a 48-foot sportfisherman on a dark canal.

They hanged Captain Kidd, didn't they? But they let Anne Bonny off.

Tonight, My mission: Piracy, just like them. Swoop down. Grapple the treasure. Sail Away on the high seas. A Privateer strike, with no warning.

Halloween, the perfect night. 4 a.m. The shades closed in to ebony, total darkness. A symphony. Dressed in costume like Black Bart; a cardboard cutlass, my fingers clutched a three foot-long set of bolt-cutters and twin jumper cables. Pirates' tools. Yacht-grabbers' weapons.

Deadly quiet. The sweet scent of honeysuckle hung heavy in moist, ocean air. Suddenly, twin headlights swept into the shadowed alley-way. My heart thumped. A prowl car, two hundred feet away, bright beams probing. I froze, head down, brain churning, vibrating with crazy, unspeakable horror images. Prison. Prison food. Five-to-ten, no parole. Yeah, they hanged Captain Kidd for Piracy, didn't they. Hung his body up 'til it rotted.

Blackbeard – they shot him, sabered him, beheaded him. We made Johnny Depp a Star? Errol Flynn, before? I blinked an eye at my watch, not moving, praying forgiveness. My mind raced wildly: But where was

Bradbury Kornbloom? What the buccaneer was I doing in this plot?

Yeah — I was there to play Pirates of Pens-Ants with this boat.

Me? Plunder a $500,000 yacht? Insanity. Okay, I could lust in my heart for treasures I'll never have—a wild spree with a Brittany starlet, a Ferrarri roadster, an unlimited platinum American Express card, a winning lottery ticket— but my follow-through — more like tweaking an extra bite-size Almond Joy from the Dentist's office; I'd be saddled with guilt for a week. Hijacking a half-mil$ yacht-goodie? Starkly beyond my wildest fantasy. A nightmare. But my buddy Bradbury C. Kornbloom demanded the absolute. The panic in his voice said he wasn't pulling my leg. What he begged for was – grand larceny. Grand Piracy. No guts, no gravy. I craved a flagon of grog.

His world came crashing down with his divorce, a bizarre tale. Korny's never-loving spouse of three years – his second, whom I'll call Lady – waltzed out on him and sued for divorce in New York City. She petitioned for "Possession of Domicile," which in this case was the booty, a 48-foot, twin screw Egg Harbor, not new, almost paid for, swaddled with radar, sat-nav, depth sounders, single side-band, GPS, RDF, 007, you name it. Yacht was his sole asset; only monetary value he had in the marriage, but..

The Court nodded sympathetically to the poor chick. Well didn't it let Anne Bonny loose? Awarded her possession of domicile, plus $200 a week alimony to tide her, while the judiciary ground through legalities. That takes a while in frantic ol' NY. They missed the secrets, the whole truth of who she was. I'll divulge that little gem (ha-ha) as we get to it, later.

Anne Bonny's ruse was to plead preggers; went to jail anyway. The fiasco -- Annie two-timed her lover Calico Jack Rackham, with female pirate Mary Read. That was frowned on even a hundred years ago. Annie conned the judges, played on sympathy, finally dropped out of history. Delivered the kid? Speculation, her father came, for a new pristine life. Fat chance, in Merry Old England.

Kornbloom's procedings snagged in NYC lingering for months. Meanwhile, Lady hired a crew of eye-patched riffaff, cast off, hove domicile down the Big Ditch to Lauderdale, Kornbloom's "Ft. Lewd." Also, out of NYC jurisdiction, yo-ho-ho and a bucket of Grey Goose grog. More twists and turns.

Contempt of court? Possible an All-American wife and non-mother would tempt Contempt? So, the boat was absent, gone; left Kornbloom sucking his thumb. Case finally made the docket, Lady cried her eyes out so the judge ruled, "You poor, disadvantaged little woman, you can sell the domicile and give Korney his half."

That would be minus, of course, the two grand or so in alimony payments the slob hadn't been contributing. Would the truth ever out?

Wasn't over yet. Kornbloom, who had signed away all rights when he said "I do," was sleeping in his car for a couple of months, so one more body blow wouldn't rate a collapse. He waited, patiently – catatonically. But patience was a virtue. A quirk in the

Big Apple's court dictated the divorce to take nine more months. Technically, Korney/Lady would be married until deep into the new millenium, at least into next yacht season. Judge, in infinite wisdom, cast a final date by which she must sell the yacht and divvy up.

Fat chance, as any fool would realize about a woman Privateer's attitude on property. Sell her domicile? Give that slob her money? He could just suck wind.

As time slipped on, all Korney heard was grapevine chatter: Lady cruising as guest-cook aboard a 125-footer in the Vee-Is, sporadically visiting Ft. Lewd and the said domicile, name of *Captive*; not *Queen Anne's Revenge*. He didn't know where the boat of contention was.

His attorney – after a full day of brow-knitting at $350 an hour -- the ambulance- woofer pronounced the only way to get leverage: Get the boat back to Big Apple's jurisdiction.

Korney called me, sobbing.

"Yo, my ol' buccaneer buddy," he whimpered, " you gotta help me steal it back."

"I am not a crook," I answered, quoting someone I remember was not George Washington.

"But," he retorted, "Could we be convicted of plundering my own boat?" Sure of himself in the clinches, Bradbury Kornbloom. Perhaps.

How could we bring sense to this nonsense?

Is Boatnapping a Sin, God? Please don't look!

The boat, Korney related, was stashed in the Miami-Fort. Lauderdale area. "Hey, just check out the canals   until you find her. You remember, she's an Egg Harbor,   flybridge, white, tuna-tower, blue cove stripe. You know, an individual. A standout."

Sure, how many canals, a zillion, in Miami to Lauderdale and between. And maybe Egg Harbor sportfishers stand out in the Hudson backwaters,   but two zillion flybridges poke up on fun- fishing yachets against the skyline of El Gold Coast. Question was, whose boat was it? Since he bought it and paid every cent of the mortgage in five years, what was her claim, from just saying "I do."

But then Anne Bonny never asked, just took what was there. And she sequestered six years in the pokey for it. They didn't behead women pirates.

To find that whisker-pole in a haystack could burn up enough fuel – I'd get a hero medal from OPEC. But our friendship of 20 years had him blubbering on long distance. Okay, I'd tackle the Johnny Depp scene. Soon-est. Promise.

What? Easier than I could dream. Was ESP flow-ing in my veins? I did remember *Captive*. Driving home from the Seminole Casino on Saturday, counting my winnings with my free hand, glancing out the window down a wide canal that juts off the ICW, right off down-town Ft.Lewd.

Suddenly. There! Bellied up to the bar, avast, be-hind a coral rock condo, in the company of strangers. Hendricks Isle. Merely one of many.

This dolly, I knew her. Parked the car, sidled up to her and saw she was sad, waif-like, not in the best of shape, looked sorely used. It was her— she— *Captive*.

I wandered along the dock with clever questions of hangers-on, like a P.I., with veiled eyelids. "Hey you think that Egg Harbor is for sale ?" CSI I'm not, but eventually I found out; Lady came in about once a week. She had a friend nearby. Some yo-yo beach boy no doubt, but she was spending most of her time there, not here. I also saw there were live-aboard boats around *Captive*, docked bow-to, with a finger pier running alongside. The canal, after a few interesting wiggles, emptied into the ICW. My heart leapt as I realized, three bridges away from that dock was the open ocean; the beautiful blue Gulfstream. Buccaneer blood pulsed in my temples.

I phoned Korney and laid the good news on him, but explained the main problems would be: 1) Finding Lady not at home, long enough to pull off the caper. 2) Getting past the padlocks on the boat and starting the engines. 3) Not waking up other boat owners sleeping ten feet away. Otherwise, a piece of baba au rum-cake.

If Disaster Strikes, Is it worse than Grapeshot Salvos?

Poor Korney arrived Friday and I saw trauma had taken a terrible toll. He'd lost weight. His eyes were two fried eggs badly in need of a Bloody Mary.

I tried to take his mind off the operation, which my former buddies in the CIA, from whom I had taken the liberty of begging advice, dubbed this "The Yacht Custody Caper." We got to a supermarket for supplies on the trip home. We'd have to take it offshore as much as possible to stay clear of the Coast Guard, Marine Patrol, Customs, and Water Police abounding in certain metro areas, due in large part to many other types of marine activities occuring here on early mornings.

Besides, we'd be aboard a readily identifiable commodity. *Captive* would have to be deface-lifted.

"What do you eat?" I asked him, but it was obvious he had not been thinking about food for about three months. His clothes hung on him like borrowed from Big Doo-Daddy. "What about some Egg-Os? Spam? Canned chili? Beer? Vodka? Bacardi Rum?" I asked.

Nothing made much impression. I sent him off to buy charts, while I rounded up bolt-cutters, screw-drivers, pliers, wrenches, and a cache of Brugal Rum. I also packed in a supply of paint remover, plastic letters, and masking tape for which I had very special plans.I met Korney at the apartment we rented a block away from the locus we were now calling "F-Dock Zero."

Sitting on the floor sketching the escape route on charts, something in his eyes reminded me of a cloistered inmate, basket weaving. I didn't want to rumple him, but we had to talk.

"*Scenarios*," I whispered gently, not to upset him.

"What do you mean, scenarios?"

"I want to play 'What If'-- Like this:"

Scenario Uno: We slip up to the dock at 4 a.m., swiftly climb aboard, break the cabin door padlocks with the bolt cutters, jump start engine, release the docklines. Slip silently into the mists. Time: 2.2 minutes.

Korney was all smiles.

Scenario Dos: We slip into the boat and the batteries dead. Won't start. Engines won't even groan for us.

"I got a jump-charger!" offers Korney.

"Okay, but just in case, we need a little outboard standing off to give us a tow." I called a few friends, lined up a guy I know with an outboard. He will stand by his phone at midnight, and if we give him the word, He'll show up.

Scenario Tres: We are standing in the cockpit with the engines clicking over, ready to cast off. Lady shows up with her beach-boy to spend the night.

"We break his legs," Korney sniggled, but he didn't smile. I de-escalated him to "forcibly restraining" said boy-bum while I back the boat out.

Scenario Quatro: Neighbor on sailboat next door wakes up and spots us lurking in the cockpit with bolt cutters.

"We tell him Lady lost her key to padlock. She is joining us later for a cruise to Bahamas."

"At four a.m. in the morning? Who's gonna believe that? What if he tries to stop us?"

"We break his legs."

"No."

Korney hashed it over, knitting his brow, rolling his fried-egg eyes. "I got it. I am a Deputy U.S. Marshall and we are repossessing this yacht under orders of the Court of New York."

"At 4 a.m. wearing cut-off blue jeans and Top-Siders?"

"Undercover agents from the DEA Drug Enforcement Bureau?"

Better. Not bad. Could work, I admitted. He unfolded a copy of his last court summons, with official stamps, whereases and all. Maybe divorce turned Korney into the con man of the ICW. We now had escalated into the Over-the-Canal Gang.

Johnny Depp never had to put up with this.

The plan, foolproof. We were about to re-po Korney's $hundred-plus-grand rubber duckie. The minutes ticked by as we ground our teeth in the apartment, awaiting H-hour. Korney gulped Valiums. I was eyeing the bottle of rum; Maybe I should have sprung for a brace of those liter-and-a-half jugs. At midnight we staked out *Captive*. All dark. Lady's parking space was empty. I hit a payphone and dialed my friend with the outboard. It rang twenty times. Finally his girlfriend picked it up. She hissed: "If that is you Malcolm, I am not answering!" I cut her off, panicked. "Wait! I am Mack's friend. He was supposed to meet me with his outboard." The line was silent for a long time. "Hey, are you there? The outboard..."

"My outboard is not going anywhere tonight. And if you see Malcolm..."

I hung up the phone. The first reef won't move.

I gave Korney the bad news. He was unbent. I couldn't tell by his expression, though, if he was alert or trance-posed. His eyes did not blink.

"We are going," he blabbered. "Backup or no backup. *Captive* gets her freedom tonight!"

Okay. Three a.m. Time to make a final reconnoiter. I checked the view. Nothing. We moved to the dock and slithered around, checking lines, finger-waving for wind, Studying the glazed surface for tide. I moved in close to the boat to make sure. Suddenly my foot nudged something soft, right next to *Captive*. It leaped up, barking its head off. A dog! Geez, the sailboat next door had a dog.

I froze. Whispered, "Nice doggie." I scrounged in my jacket pocket and fished out half a tootsie roll. Rover gurgled and snapped his thanks. I scrambled back to Korney to unveil the latest. Not only did we not have an outboard backup, an unfriendly pooch that could turn into a very loud watchdog. Other than that, we'd clear on schedule.

"Do not worry about dogs, "Korney stage-whispered back. We will bribe him with a sirloin steak if we have to. And besides, I've got this special rapport with members of the canine race."

A Tale of the Dog, not Morning After

Near four a.m., it was time to make our move, as my CIA guys had counseled. Korney drove me to the boat in a rented car. A guy carrying bolt cutters and jumper cables might be a little suspect walking down a residential marina street in the middle of the night. Take no chances. He dropped me off, I hid in the alley shadows while he stashed the car in a safe spot. Long before the stroke of dawn, we, praying to the spirit of Long John Silver, we'd be on our way to Manhattan Towers.

Now here I was, breathing rapidly. This was the moment the twin-orb headlights appeared on the dark street, briefly flashing mid-day into my hiding place. Inside the prowl car were two of Broward County's finest, taking care of business. My tongue was dry as a bone. "Local Yacht Captain dies of fright under bush in Ft. Lauderdale."

The car eased past. My sanity oozed back. Where the hell was Bradbury Kombloom?

"Psst, "He whispered from behind the bush.

I jumped almost straight up. The dog loomed out

of the darkness, teeth bared. I pulled out a package from my pocket, a five buck slice of Virginia Country Ham, and waved it at him. It broke my heart, but a tootsie roll is not chewy enough.

Poochie wolfed at it like an audition for Purina Dog Chow, whimpering happily.

Korney leaned over to give him a friendly pat.

"Nice doggy." Poochie sniffed at Kornbloom's shoe, edged in close, lifted his leg, and relieved himself of half a liter. Korney did indeed have rapport with wild animals.

Too Stunned to move before it hit him, he tried to nail the dog with his Top-Sider. His language was unprintable. The pooch waddled off, satisfied, the ham dangling from its jaws.

I grabbed Kornbloom, propelled him toward the boat, and jammed the bolt cutters in his paws. He climbed on board, swiping at his pants leg with a Kleenex.

Time to move, and fast. I started with dock lines, unwrapping double folds, when suddenly there was a crash like somebody had dropped a giant pair of bolt cutters on a fiberglass teak deck. Yeah. Korney was cussing, not softly. I held my breath. Two of us yelling, even at each other, wouldn't work. Then finally, the crack of the bolt cutters as the padlock snapped. Korney's footsteps moved into the saloon.

Hours ticked past; my Rolex dragged out only seconds. Kornbloom poked his head out. Smirked. "The starter — disconnected. I had to stick the wire back on."

"Okay," I whispered. "Hit it." A cold trickle of sweat slid down my back. Next door, I could hear the sailboat's clock chiming loud as Big Ben. The night, still. My heart pumped in my chest like a dribbled basketball. Will he never? Korney's head popped out of the big doors, slowly shaking from side to side.

"What? Why aren't we going?"

"Throttles are handled from the tower."

Korney had installed this unique— or stupid— system, to prevent theft. I'd have to go up on the tower and work the throttles. It looked about half a mile to the top; every boat in the canal and half the condos could spot me.

Korney stage whispered, "Out of gear, then idle right after it fires. Got it?"

I pulled the gearshift knob out. Pushed the throttles on full. Suddenly I heard the grinding of the starters. Big twin diesels roared with a thunder that echoed up and down the silent harbor. Were lights popping on in every boat and condo? No. But the boat was moving. I looked down at the length of white fiberglass below me. Captive was trying to climb up on the dock!

 The damned boat was in gear! I fumbled with the gearshift. Korney rushed up the ladder, surefooted as an orangutan, hand over hand.

"Pull the damn knob out! Pull it out!" He yanked it almost off the console and the boat grumbled, then slowly stopped surging. Korney's face was ashen, even in the pale light of predawn. We waited, breathlessly, for the uproar to begin, for yachtsmen and condo dwellers to charge out and start beating us with gaff poles.

Nothing. These people could sleep through a Rap-Smash concert.

I eased down the ladder, knees playing drumbeat paradiddles against each other. I didn't yelp when Korney planted a size 12 on my fingers. The cockpit seemed hours away. I hadn't had this hazardous a trip since I was sent to the masthead by Ted Turner during a racing storm, to untangle a halyard.

Korney showed me: First the power cord, then the dock lines. He swung back up the ladder to steer from above. On the dock, the stable concrete felt good. I unscrewed the power line— so far so good.

Then, bent over, I felt a pointed nudge in a very tender portion of my anatomy. Very insistent. No voice, no sound. What? A gun? It shoved harder. Turn around or fall flat? Then, hot breath panting against my rump. The dog's nose was poked up my crotch. More ham, he panted.

"Nice poochie," I whispered. He lifted his leg. I dodged in time.

Tossed the power cord into the cockpit and slipped the dock lines. Two seconds. They were uncleated. I high-signed Kornbloom.

The big engines grumbled, but the boat waddled backwards. We were about to commit pillage! Piracy without a shot fired! Edging down the narrow canal, we passed a raucous Halloween party behind one of the condos. They had not heard us; nor we them.

A couple of turns, twists, and wiggles; we gave the first bridge the toot signal, one prolonged and a short. The arches swung open and we triumphantly made our getaway, skull and crossbones forever!

Korney and I broke into smiles. High fives. Then

the second bridge, same toots. We waited. Nothing. A couple more blasts, more insistently. No answer.

Korney quickly lapsed into frantic. Marooned between two bridges, it could be only seconds until a Marine Patrol boat would be snapping our heels.

"Pull over to that restaurant dock," I yelled. I hopped off the bow, scrambled up a steep bank at Hooters – where the party was winding down – to the bridge tender's shack. Completely dark. When did they shut down bridges at night? What about commercial traffic?

Peering inside, I saw the tender lounged back, feet propped up on the desk. His mouth open. Was he alive? Fantastic; we were committing Grand Piracy and this guy picked our night to pack it in. Then I heard snorts through the door. Gaffer was asleep!

I banged on the door. "Open the bridge! Open the rodram bridge!" Slowly he righted himself, nodded, and ambled to the controls.

I clambered down the embankment, leapt back onto *Captive* to calm Kornbloom, who was systematically shredding our charts into confetti. A real pressure Pirate, Kornbloom.

The bridge trundled open and we were through. Only one more to go before we were loosed upon the world.

Then we heard it; a high pitched wailing somewhere behind us. Siren. Smack down the arrow-straight ICW. We strained to make it out. Then, a bright blue light, flashing, just atop a screaming bow wave. Cops. We'd been had; the Marine Patrol bearing down on us. What's our plan now, Black Bart?

Kornbloom dived for the lower cabin, ordering me to the wheel. We cannot outrun a cop-boat. Since the drug runners, they all drive gofast Cigarettes. We were doomed. I gently eased back on the throttles. No sense in making it tougher. Water patrol bearing down on us, not one but two bow waves bouncing a couple of hundred yards back. They've got us dead to rights.

Korney struggled up from the cabin, a sheaf of papers clutched in his hand. A stricken look. "I got the ship's papers. I can prove it's my own boat." He rummaged through them, tossing letter-sized chunks from one end of the salon to the other. The twin bow waves were now astern, flying, siren screaming.

But only one siren. Only one flashing blue light

Suddenly they were alongside. We were smacked by the wake of the first boat, then the second. Thunderous noise assailed our ears. And then they were past. Stunned, we watched after them for ten seconds before it hit us.

Cops chasing a doper! We were merely almost in their way. A laugh bubbled out of my mouth, and suddenly Kornbloom and I were hugging each other. The closest call has turned out to be a false alarm after all.

Now we were through the third bridge, almost to open ocean. The bridge tender would jot down our yacht name as we passed through. That is all Lady would know; *Captive* escaped to sea, into the Atlantic at 0428 hours, Sunday. Happy Halloween...

But we were not completely out of it yet. Important work to do before daylight. We pulled into a pre-arranged private slip along the ICW. In seconds we were

tied up and Korney was down below, dredging up female clothes, draperies, dishes, the family silver pattern,
and sundry items Lady could have him hung for. All of
this to be stashed in plastic bags, left on the patio of the
cohort's house, to be transported to the Greyhound Bus
station, and a large locker. Nothing to make positive iden-
tification for Lady was left aboard. I sweated, struggled,
loading on the balance of our provisions, unloading lady's
gear. How can one woman store that many shoes, clothes,
in two little hanging lockers. Korney was digging in the
small grey cabinet, pulling out handfuls of fancy folded
papers.

"What's that?" I asked.

"Stock certificates. She kept them on the boat."

"Huh?" I grazed through them. Five thousand shares
AT&T, a load of IBM, Getty Oil, Standard Oil, Florida
Power and Light, an aged flock of some little computer
company called Microsoft.

"Hey, a lot of money is tied up here. These all
Lady's?"

"Yeah." He crammed them sourly into a plastic bag.
"You didn't know, did you. She's worth a couple mil
and a quarter bucks, stocks and bonds. A present from
her first and former husband. He's dead now. Live and
learn."

(Ha-ha)! What I had meant to tell you. Truth at last
about the "poor abandoned chick" secret.

I was speechless. So little Lady had figured her prize
this time down the aisle was a used yacht, which she
could easily have bought new, a hundred times over.
Wealth begets wealth. Any tinge of sympathy for her went

screaming out my ears. But finally we had stowed all our gear and piled all of her things on the patio.

Sun streaked across the horizon as we shoved off, joining the throng of charter boats roaring out to sea for the day's fishing In no time we had broken off from the covey of sportfishers and were pounding north, ten, twenty, thirty miles offshore, running wild and loose. One more chore I had to complete before we were out of the woods, and I hung upside down over the stern for a couple of hours doing it But at last it was finished.

Back into the main salon where Kornbloom was about to break out the happy juice in celebration of our success, when I saw it on the horizon, a white-hot, pin-point, bright searchlight, so strong it was visible miles away in the early daylight. The cold worm crawled up my brain again, the one that told me we were about to be snatched back to reality. Coast Guard.

"Well Korney, old Corsair, we almost got away with it. But there they are, a Coast Guard helichopper bearing down on us a thousand miles an hour, soon to be followed, no doubt, by a hundred foot cutter, with twin fifty caliber machine guns trained on us."

I took the big bottle of Bacardi and tipped it up. "Well, you can run but you cannot hide," as Muhammad Ali, or John Paul Jones, used to say.

Kornbloom was grimly staring straight ahead. I could see the wheels of fortune churning in his head. He was not going to give up without a struggle. We had not come this far to lie down on the mat. "We'll scuttle the ship if they try to take us alive." He dived into the main cabin and opened a hatch. He fumbled with a big valve.

"Hey, wait one minute!" I yelled, abandoning the wheel, grabbing his arms. "Let's at least wait until we're sure. Thirty miles offshore! I do not fancy walking the plank, sinking slowly into the east 'til I am dead nuts positive somebody will haul me out of the briny."

"Yeah," he grimaced wildly. "It is never over until it is over."

We climbed back to the deck just in time. The white-hot light was upon us now, traveling, it looked, at the speed of light. But instead of a C.G. chopper fifty feet off the deck, it turned out bigger than we thought, a mile in space, trailing a long green streamer.

"Whoa!" I yelled. "That is the U. S. Government alright. But not a 'copter. We're just south of Cape Canaveral! It's an Aegean missile launch!"

I pointed out the chart, our location; Korney ruefully stabbed a pinky to a small type notice: *"Missile launching area. Boatmen are warned to be on the lookout for falling rocket casings."*

"Hah!" Kornbloom shouted. "Ha? Hahahahaha! And I was on the brink of disaster, about to poke a hole and scuttle her bottom. Ah, my baby, my *Captive*, how could I think of such a thing for you!" He grabbed a magnum of champagne from the cooler. All grins. Then came another idea. His brows lit up.

I reminded him of the two hours of work I had done over the side, with a can of solvent and a bunch of paste-on letters, plus hull striping; it had forever altered her name and appearance. It was a sticky job but somebody had to do it. Even if we were spotted by an alert constabulary now, we would not be the same boat.

Nothing looked the same. Cove stripe, scrolls, everything was changed. I grinned back at him and picked up my own magnum. This was going to be a free-boot to remember. Never make the evening news.

"So! Ho! Wait a minute!" he shouted. "The whole entire solution just comes to me!"

"What?"

"Her name was never on this title. I have always owned this boat. She can't sell it because it was never hers! Regardless of what some judge in the Big Apple said, My name is on the title, and I am sellimg this boat. Not today! No! Six months ago!"

"What in the every-loving blue-eyed world are you…" I started…

"I am selling this boat to You! Right now! We will confirm the date of sale when we get to St. Thomas in the Vee-Eyes!"

"But the judge…" I offered.

"The judie is in New Yawk! The boat has been sold in St.Thomas, U.S.Virgin Islands! Six months ago! It is retroactive. I have worked it all out in my head. The boat is gone. It has a new name, a new owner, and she can't protest because she took it out of the New Yawk Court Jurisdiction! And it wasn't even hers!"

"You're sure of that?"

"You got a better idea? Now, swing that helm around on a course of Sou' by Sou' East. We are sailing this Pirate Galleon over the Spanish Main, down to Far Tortuga, the Virginie Isles! Today we have become the gen-yew-wine modern Pirates of the Caribbean Sea!" Laughing hysterically, he uncorked the big magnum of champagne. We drank to bachelor-hood. We drank to the U.S. of Coast Guard; to the Aegea of missiles. We even drank to Lady, who must deserve a heaping thimble-full of sympathy in her chicanery, and loss.

And at last we drank to our new Pirate's Prize, as she picked her way steadily southward, with her new paint job, and her new name:

Not Blackbeard's *Queen Anne's Revenge*, but our own christening...

--Free-N-E-Zee--

\#

CAPT. CHUCK GNAEGY

Two

Pirates in Caribbean History

Anne Bonny, the most famous female Pirate, married James Bonny, a brigand who tried to steal her father's plantation and was reputedly a snitch for Nassau Governor Woodes Rogers; who utimately put an end to that phase of Piracy in the Caribbean. She tired of her hubbie's traitorous behavior and took up with Calico Jack Rackham, Captain of the Revenge; but she also had a dalliance with Pirate Mary Read, a reported Lesbian union. Wearing men's clothes they fought with cutlass and pistol. The Governor of Jamaica dispatched a gunboat to capture them all. Both women, in spite of their supposed Lesbian union, claimed they were pregnant, and were tried separately from the men. No record was found of a birth to either woman. Mary Read died from malaria, while Anne later recieved a pardon and disappeared from Pirate history. One story claims she reunited with her father and led a normal life. No proof of that in current files. But following is a story of a modern female entrepeneur in the Isles of Pirates.

Delilah & the Healin' Hole
Ponce de Leon Passed Up a Fortune

Pale moonlight streamed onto my Round Robin, as I nosed her slowly between the bar and the broken coral banks which edge into the harbor at North Bimini. The twin cats purred, happy as a bowl of Cheerios, burbling along at idle. But then I realized their eight-string hums were matched by another, not quite as loud but equally satisfied set of steady rhythmic thrumming. I eased off the wheel and slipped out of the deckhouse to check. Could a surprise visitor be slipping up my stern? But no, it was Delilah.

She was mounded up on the afterdeck, pink and pretty as a Virgin Island sunrise, and snoring fit to call up a gathering of Galapagos walruses. I chuckled at the harmonics, eased back into the steering station. She was the reason I was there; Delilah, and Ponce de Leon.

And a million bucks.

Now I am normally a pretty straight ahead guy, happy for the success of friends. My usual state of near-poverty only bothers me sometimes, like at night, when I spend a whole day in the City and do not once get asked for "a little change." Puzzles me that some have it and I don't, even when we started out together on the same project. At this point, however, I felt fine about Delilah, for she had let me into our imminent, soon to come genuine prosperity..

It got its start at three ayem, doesn't everything, when my phone jangled in the velvet black dark, tearing me back from a dream of six coeds on a skinny-snorkeling tour. I wasn't sure they were gone when I murmured into the line, and was answered by a throaty, soft, female voice. She wanted to charter my boat for a trip to the islands. Never-never land never felt so promising. I assured her, "Captain Chuck is always ready for ... adventure. Now, about the charter fee..."

"Capitano Chucko," the sweet voice offered, "this is a no-fee charter. But it is gonna make you a million bucks!"

Now while I had known a few young ladies of promise – for things they never intended to deliver — this one sounded like true blue, and a million bucks these days was not without the realm of reason, even if I don't play basketball. Still, the ogre of suspicion hovered.

"Uh, why don't you tell me more about the, uh, million bucks." I stumbled, hiding the suspicion that I may be the victim of an obscenely cruel hoax by an IRS Agent.

"Hah! Most important find in the history of the world! Need I say more?""Well, I remember, way back in the dark ages, that is what Timothy Leery thought about lysergic acid, but it turned out to be worse than caffeine. Uh, who is...?"

"It is so important that I cannot even tell you on the phone, Loverboy. I am coming right over."

Click. The obscene phone promiser hung up.

But then, from the dim recesses of my memory the little quirk in her voice came back to identify itself. Yes. M-hmm. Evening News. Without a doubt. Katie Couric. I would recognize that voice anywhere. But why? Hell, I thought, if I am not still dreaming, this better make sense when she gets here. Katie Couric. A million bucks. She knows where the bucks are buried. My mind boggled.

I staggered into the galley and rattled the coffee pot out of hibernation. Why should it sleep when I cannot. I was trying blindly to comprehend the mysteries of life — why do people crave Beluga caviar? Why is it always darkest before dawn? Why would a raving celebrity like Katie Couric want to see me in the wee hours of the night? But I soon got the answer to at least one of them. She rushed in breathlessly and overflowed onto my couch. It was not K.C. Not even a look-alike.

"Delilah!" I should have guessed.

"Are you ready for this, Captain Chucko? I have found it! Eureka, as Isaac Newton said when the apple smacked him."

"You have found what? Laws of gravity are already written down in the good book."

"I have found what mortal man has been seeking since the first millenium dawned on us." She gurgled as though she had found a market for belly button lint.I clutched my coffee cup and sank down into a chair. "Oookay. What?"

The Fountain of Youth.

Delilah was a whirlwind of a lady who steamed in and out of my sphere at irregular intervals, trailing sparks like Halley's Comet. Whatever she touched turned out to be a Fellini movie; no less bizarre than the lady herself. For as much of her as there was overflowing my couch, there could have been several others.

When she was born, she must have been tiny and loveable, a bundle of sweetness and light wrapped in butttons and bows. The problem was s feeding her.

Everything was grist, as they say. Food for the winter, all year. Delilah was now a shimmering 300 poun bowl of jello with pink skin stretched over it. And jolly — joie d'vivre by the wheelbarrow full. But, Obese. When she was in the water steaming around my boat, I was afraid someone would send for Capt. Ahab, or GreenPeace would come thundering down, waving banners. The first time she chartered my Round Robin, to snorkel the reefs, I was sure she couldn't hoist her watermelons back onto the deck, and that I'd have to tow her ashore and nudge her up onto the beach. She solved that by suggesting we rig a bosun's sling at the halyard, to winch her up like a bill of lading.

In her spare time she was a lady wrestling promoter, with friends such as Jesse Ventura, Hillary, Howard Stern, Cher, whose voices she also loved to imitate. She herself is a legendary character who seems trapped in perpetual Halloween.

Yet she's loveable, though living proof that big ideas come in giant economy size. With her own plans on how the world should run; how life should be lived.

"Uh, the Fountain of Youth?" I mumbled. "I always thought it was some well-wisher's imagination..."

"You got it, Capitan Chucko. Fountain of Youth, as Chris Colon once said, "I have found it!"

"But Delilah, if you will forgive me for being so, uh, direct, You, um, haven't changed that much. I mean, always looked uh, younger than me, but…"

"I haven't been there yet, you handsome sea dog. That is why I am here. I want you to take me there!"

"Well, sweet lady, if I knew where, I think maybe I would have already made that voyage."

She lifted a delicate pinky. "You are putting me on, as usual, good Capitano. Of course you don't know. But I do. I have a map! From the Pirate Edward Cheeks!"

"That's Teach," I corrected, "Blackbeard."

She chuckled, a tremor from down deep inside her, that swelled and reverberated like watching Mt. Etna go bloombo bloombo. "The place that gushes with the elixir of life; it is right in the middle of the ocean. It is in …Bin-i-mi!"

"Bin-i-mi! Bim-ini?" I said. "Bimini."

"So you already knew. And you did not even tell me. You devil." She giggled, jiggling my entire couch.

"Well, no, I didn't know. I don't know anything. Where is this Pirate map?" "It is right here. Just look at this!" She waved the crude, hand drawn diagram. "The natives knew about this for centuries, but they are afraid to go there. A fresh water wishing well, right in the back yard of their island. And they think it is haunted. But the water will heal any kind of sore or sickness, and the only guy who does dip into it is already over a hundred…"

"Delilah, what in the ever loving, blue eyed…"

"And I want you to take me over there. Today! Look, love… bottled up, that agua is worth millions!" Her eyes took on a coy look as she surveyed my reaction.

"What about... halfies?"

I know Bimini, of course. It is always coming up famous in some strange way, not unlike Delilah herself. Ponce de Leon stopped there looking for his Fountain of Youth, sure, and Pirates hung out there lurking for treasure ships to pass, but there was no fresh water; so they moved on to Nassau. One-time denizen Ernie Hemingway wrote a book about it; ESP prophet Edgar Cayce predicted that Atlantis would rise again offshore of it, though it's only a little strip of sand and gumbo-limbo trees about a mile long.

Big fat marlin-hunting Ryboviches and Hatteri full of heavy wallets kept the island from sliding into the Gulfstream by stuffing money up its economy; and later on, during moonlight nights, high speed Cigarettes zoomed past on what looked like a regular schedule, while pounds of gold chains began to decorate natives who shuffled on down its one narrow avenue with know-ing eyes — the grass/cocaine connection. A glittering past, yes.

It would take my Round Robin an hour or two to get there, even over-loaded with Pink Delilah. This all fit right in with five hundred years of Pirates, plunder-ers, and fast buck chasers. Maybe we're next in line.

But some things do not change. Bonefish Basil Bottomley, for one thing, had not changed in all the years I have been cruising into the wild and wonderful world of the Bahama Islands. Perhaps he didn't change for a considerable number of years before that.

Okay then, it was Bonefish Basil Bottomley I would ask about this impossible dream. After all, it's Delilah's nickel. I'd leave her napping to go find him. But half way to Bonefish Basil's digs, I chickened out. Cold feet crept inside my topsiders. Was this damn foolishness or what? Hunting some strange hocus pocus magic bullet in the middle of this fisherman's paradise? Swept along on Delilah's boundless enthusiasm, was I a victim of a crueler hoax than the IRS trap? If his name was Bonefish Basil, maybe mine was Bonehead Chuck.

How could anything be around this long and not be famous, I wondered. Is anything left to discover anymore, not on the moon? But then I remembered the guy who forgot to look under his own nose. He kept a big metal doorstop around for about seventy-five years because it was heavy. After he died, his nephew sliced a chunk off and had it analyzed. It was pure silver. Or the guy who found a big green rock in his bag of coffee beans – a 25-carat emerald, genuine Colombian. So okay, miracles do happen. But hardly ever, if then, to somebody like me who spends his life in quiet desperation, waiting for the lottery ticket that never ka-chings.

But Bonefish Basil did not laugh. He turned the crude diagram over in his grizzled hand. "De Fontin of Yout?" he says. "Mon, dis place here on dis map, it be de Healin' Hole. You want to go dere?"

"Uh, the Healin' hole?" I got a feeling he had been there once or twice, and was on the verge of giving me a spiel.

"Yeh. Mon, it heal everytin'. I show you. Two humdred fifty dolluh.."

Mmm. Yes. The ills of the world, all healed, only $250. I've had the same proposition in Coconut Grove, or South Beach. But Bonefish Basil is a man who works for his money. I know him. He knows me. He was not overdosed on cowpath toad stools, or cracked coka canes. His normal occupation is luring white-necked tourists to shallow waters around these scrubby islands, called flats, where a silvery, ghost-like creature hi-jacks fishing gear from unsuspecting anglers, and occasionally rewards one of them with the thrill of his life, tearing off two hundred yards of line in screaming runs before succumbing, to wind up as a painted stuffed memento on Strother P. Mongrue's rec-room wall.

But to Bonefish Basil Bottomley it is only a job. And so is guiding us to the "Fontin of Yout'."

So, it was there, after all. And at least one Bahamian has known about it all the time. I began to wonder about Bonefish Basil. I knew he has been here since year one, and he was not a young man. Shiny black, with leathery skin the color of oiled mahogany and textured like baked driveway asphalt. I knew his reputation for delivering the goods, and he would do his best for us. Delilah's two plastic gallon jugs, in their crate, were ready to go.I gently shook Delilah out of the land of Wynken Blynken & Nod, where she had become an island curiosity snoring on my back deck, and led her down the main drag, dodging '57 Chebbies and brand new motobikes and golf carts that— although the whole stretch is only a quarter mile long— zoom endlessly back and forth.

We were followed by a clutch of children and old folks who were watching Delilah so intently I expected any moment one would proclaim her Goddess of the Volcano. People who have lived on an island all their lives learn to appreciate size. Sure, ever see those movies of Hawaii? Delilah could easily be borne on a festooned litter, by two dozen strapping young warriors; and a eunuch with a palm frond, shooing flies.

Bonefish Basil, on the other hand, was not as awestruck as he was stunned. He glanced warily at his new passenger, measuring the place she would fit into his worm-eaten blue skiff, which was only kept in one piece by endless coats of paint that held it together. I expected any minute the price was going up, for extra ballast – er, cargo. He looked worried, his aging brows furrowed in a double dip.

"We gon need to go on de high tide, mon. We gon need plenty watuh to get across dot bank today." He sucked in his breath as Delilah -heaved herself delicately over the gunnel and oozed onto a seat. "You gon take care a mah money now, mon?"

Delilah chortled and peeled off 5 fifties from a roll she had tucked in her considerable cleavage.

"I'll bet a good man like you'd make fifty bucks an hour in the right place, Bonefish?" Rubbed an ample hip against him, an obesely obscene gesture

Bonefish shuddered. Not a man to move mountains, or the Sea Goddess,mumbled, "Whatever you tink, mu'um. But we got to go now." His adam's apple clucked slowly up and down.

I shoved a brace of battered minnow buckets out of the way and gingerly settled myself on the forward bench seat. I knew the ride across the flats would be tricky, top-heavy with a zillion jiggling spoonsful of jello ambrosia aboard. Delilah had commandeered both swivel fishing chairs and was riding with a huge grin on her face. We cleaved the water and mushed, wallowing from the marina at the old Brown's Dock and onto the clear sparkling shallows. It was a short and easy ride, until we pulled up to a little mangrove island.

Bonefish stabbed an oar into the white sand and tied a line off. Bahama bonefish anchor-style.

"De healin' hole right in dere," Bonefish said. "We gon walk over dis here flat to get dere."

He eased out of the skiff and sank half way to his hips in the sugar-soft sand. He was eyeing Delilah. "I tink we gon have to tink of sometin now. Dis sand, it suck you right on down. Sometin heavy jus' ain't gonna make it dere."

There was not a trace of doubt, however, on Delilah's cherubic face. She had come to play. She lurched toward the gunnel and the boat ripped sickeningly to one side. Salt water flooded in like a Busch Beer commericial.

"Ohmaga!" Bonefish blurted, then swallowed hard and sloshed toward her. "Dis fine lady, she gon careen mah boat! Hol' her now!"

But he was too late. Delilah's pendulous champs were already over the side and the poor stricken skiff was showing its bottom paint to the sky. In a giant whoosh she was suddenly released, floundering in the water, flailing her ham-like arms, trying to regain her footing and equilibrium. But true to form, the sand gurgled and sucked and in seconds we knew we were in deep trouble.

"Ohmaga! Mon, you girlfren she gon' down! She gon disappear. We gon lose her! She cain't nevuh swim back up outa dot quicksand !"

Delilah had a look of stark determination on her face, but her voice was little girlish as she yelped "Help!" I surveyed the possibilities in a flash, and there were few. If I got under her to push, I did not like where I might end up. If I climbed into the boat to pull, it would be like trying to raise the Andrea Doria from a three thousand foot grave. But a faraway voice sounded in my brain: Leverage! It cried out loud at me.

I snatched the oar from its tethering stand, scooped out some loose sand, and jammed it under her ample flanks. At the same time Basil was swinging the skiff around through the swirling, frothing water. Delilah's face was ducking, and the last I saw of her was two little nostrils stretched wide open like a —excuse the simile — hippopotamus snatching a breath of air before it dove to waylay an unsuspecting Tarzan. But I was grunting like Cheetah as I tried to pry the oar under her; Bonefish was bouncing on the other side of the boat, striving to seesaw the gunnel back down. Delilah puffed like a walrus at an ice floe, chubby hands locked to the wooden rail. Suddenly there was a huge slurping pop as though the plug was pulled from the ocean, and she burst free.

"Aha!" Delilah chortled, "Not even God can sink the Titanic!"

Bonefish Basil looked done in. "Maybe you like to go on by yourself, mon."

But Delilah was not to be left sucking on her thumb. "It is my two hundred fifty bucks, Buster. I am going," she vowed, "one way or another."

So we rigged up a harness, and while Bonefish led the way, I slogged after him through sand, mud, and water, towing Delilah on her belly, a giant water toy bubbling in my wake, the jugs clanking from my shoulder.

Fifty yards inside the mangrove island, with their thousand tarantula toes stuck into the murky water, was an olympic pool-sized pond. But it was not clean and clear as the flats water. It was dank and bilious. It was cream of catfood soup.

"Dis be it, mon. De Healin' Hole. You can jes' slide on in."

I moved forward with my giant pink rubber duckie in tow, and clumsily plunged shoulder deep into the green scum. My systems shrank suddenly with a lemon pucker. It was ice water! While the flats around the Bahamas, even in winter, are so warm from the sun you think it is a salt water hot tub, this stuff was straight out of iceberg lettuce country. I yelled my displeasure.

"No need to get afraid, mon," Basil pronounced. "Dis watuh heal anyting you got wrong wit you."

I noticed he had not ventured into the arctic pool, however. He was hovering around the entrance and the hot sands.

Delilah slid off the shallow bank on her belly, gurgling happily, "Wonder what the poor people are doing today, huh, Capitan Chucko?"

"I know what one of them is doing," I replied, fervently wishing for a flock of little kids to arrive and warm up this eskimo pie. The smell of it, however, was that they had already been here and departed. The aroma was essence of green swamp.

"Look! Look!" Delilah cried. "I am floating right out of it, it is so bouyant!"[1]

Sure enough, the watermelon queen was floating with her appendages nearly high and dry, looming up like the Song of Norway bearing down in the Gulfstream. I could not help but notice that I, too, was floating higher, and with less effort than in common salt water, on only a fraction of the, excuse please – fatty tissue – as my pool mate. "What does this mean?" I wondered.

"Ho, besides that, It is not even salt water!" Delilah confided, tasting the vile green. "Take a gulp of this marvelous liqueur."

Like a dog on command, I lapped a little, terrified because I knew it was not going to heal whatever I was going to catch from it. But I found it was indeed not brine.

Now Delilah was making urmping noises, rising and sinking alternately; I knew any minute she was going to spout. She chortled gleefully, "If ol' Ponce de Leon could see us now, eh, Capitan Chucko? I am feeling younger already. I am losing years.'"

Considering the volume of green water she was displacing into the mangroves I think the Hole was also losing an essential part of itself. "You think this is something like that? It does seem pretty far fetched, doesn't it? And it smells like, uh, rotten eggs," I ventured.

"Ho! Ever whiff Hot Springs? Or the Ganges River? The sulfur baths at Rome?"

"No, but I smelled the sewer outfall from the East River once, and I cannot tell the difference."

"Sulfur is a healing potion, dear Capitan. I wager our handsome friend Bonefish Basil is never a day sick in his life. What-eh, Capitan Bottomley?"

"Yeh, I had a cold once, in grammar school," Basil answered, clearly ready, with the two hundred fifty in-pocket, to get this over with and get back home.

"I bet you don't tell us, either," Delilah says coyly, "what year you are born. How old is darling Bonefish Basil?"

"I know that alright. We all go to school here. Nineteen- twenty-eight."

"Pshaw, sweet Basil, do not kid with Delilah. I hear you are one hundred years old, even with your body of a twenty year-old."

Basil turned to me. His brows doubled up again. "I dunno what you fot lady sayin."

"I am talking Fountain of Youth, that's what. I'll bet you know about that, sweet Basil? Hmmmm?" She was convinced in her own mind, I could see that.

"Naw," Bonefish says. "Dis jes de healin hole. But now you mention it, Mistah Hemin-way, he say that, too. Say it cure his skin cancer."

"Aha! Hemingway?" Delilah was beside herself, pardon the simile. "I knew it all the time! See Capitan Chucko? We are going to bottle this stuff and we are going to be rich! Now fill up those bottles! I have seen enough to know a fortune when it runs up my nose!"

I did that, watching the green slime double-bubble into the jugs, without a doubt ending up the most fool-ish adventure in my long and distinguished career. I was considering this all the way back to Brown's Dock, while Delilah, a euphoric smile on her angel's puss, was scrib-bling madly into a large black notebook. Columns of numbers and pages of notes flowing out of her fertile pen onto the lined pages, while she occasionally glanced up at the glum expression on my weathered puss.

By the time we were back in the familiar digs of Round Robin's cabin, she had finished her note-taking and was overflowing with ideas and figures.

"See, I have it all worked out, in black and white, Capitan Chucko, and we are going to sell this marvelous brew for about twenty bucks an oh-zee— that is an ounce.

If we have to we are going to lease this whole island, or buy this spring-thing from the Bahamian Government, or whoever owns it now. Did you tell me it is haunted or was that somebody else? An advantage if it's true, because we have it all to ourselves and not any interference from the natives who might... something is bothering you about this deal?"

"Well, I uh," I stammered, "uh, don't you think you ought to have it analyzed, or checked out, or something? Shouldn't we stick it on somebody's sore finger and see what it does for them? Or somebody's bald head to see if it grows hair?"

"Ha! We already have it from the Bonefish's mouth that Ernest Hemingway found it cured his skin can..."

"Uh, Delilah, I'm sure that was Leicester. Leicester Hemingway. He was Ernest's brother. An important man himself, but he was not the author you are speaking of..."

"So we don't use his first name. I cannot see anything wrong with that. The same family." She flipped a couple of pages and scribbled notes.

Not wanting to punch a hole in her high hopes, I did not wish to pursue an argument. Who am I to fathom the nuances of a marketing scheme? But she had hit me right on the head. I wasn't sure I was the right person to be involved in this venture. She could feel it. She pinched my cheek.

"Out with it, dear boy. You'd squirm out of this?"

"Aw, Delilah, I am just a simple boat captain, you know, not exactly given to chasing after the rainbow of notoriousness. I am not even certain that I want to live forever, even if this Hole turns out to be the place ol' Ponce was looking for. The people I have seen who have passed their three score and ten do not all look too happy about it."

"Um-hummm," she says, waiting for more.

"Besides, I'm never rich in pocket money, anyway. I am just a simple man who wouldn't know what to do with a million bucks if it smacked me square in the mush..."

"So! You want I should only pay you for the charter and keep the entire damn Fountain of Youth for myself?"

I couldn't tell if she did or didn't not want me to say yes.

"I guess you are able to see right through ol' Chuck," I fumbled, admitting it.

And that was the end of it. Right there. Bango. Delilah was not a woman who would beat a dead horse, you have to hand her that. She dug down between her watermelons and pulled out a wad of hundred dollar bills. She seemed very pleased to take the entire market.

But then, Delilah was also used to dealing in big money with her wrestling promotions, and circulating with big bucks around her celebrity friends. How could a simple sea captain fit in with that life, I thought, and the answer by then was moot.

In two hours she was on Chalk's Airline speeding back to the Gold Coast with her dreams of youth water and her jugs of green unsweetened Kool-Aid, and her mountains of excess baggage, to waddle out of my life for the duration.

I was buying up all the Jamaican rum in Bimini – for Delilah was generous with her charter fee – storing up provisions for a leisurely trip "down-island" as we veteran cruisers call it.

And we both lived happily ever after, I'd like to say. Except,

Comes the reprise…

It was two years, or more, since I had taken leave of Delilah, and her memory drifted away as the spectre of most women do, when I was lolling away my time in a Bogart-type bar with ceiling fans and a wild monkey, at Puerto Plata, the Hispaniola Coast. The bartender was a ringer for Captain Jack Sparrow. I was learning rudiments of the Spanish language from an assortment of ginger-colored senoritas. I could get to the bathroom okay, and order breakfast as long as it was huevos revueltos y papas fritas – scrambled eggs and french fries – but I didn't yet have the savvy to read the best magazines. I spent a lot of time looking at pictures.

Yet there, on the front page of some gaudy-colored tabloid, printed somewhere in a foreign country, I came across a picture of this slender, sleek, model-bodied creature, a la P. Hilton, whooping it up at the birthday party of Count Di-Somebody, in Rome.

I did a very slow double take. That face. It was not Paris. But I recognized that cherubic face, that turned up nose, those glittery eyes and smiling lips. Without a doubt. But the body didn't belong there. The body on that photo was as different as Laurel was from Hardy. What was once a 10 x 10 is now sculptured to a clear, tasty Ten. I couldn't make out the headline; for while I could handle a little Spanish, this was maybe Portuguese. Or Italian. Finally I found a guy in the noisy bar at the Castillo Hotel who could read it.

I flopped into a tall rattan bar stool while he read:"Millionairess Throws Birthday Bash for Rovalty." Yeah, it looks like... but it cannot be. That slender, curvy, angular... a clear supermodel 10. It could not be. I urged the reader frantically to get past the headline, where the type was smudged and the page was torn. All he could come up with was something like

"Bottled-Water Tycoon..."

The rest was illegible. I stared at it; the face was getting younger by the minute.

I downed another shot of Brugal Rum, and stag-gered to the big mirror behind the bar. No. No such luck here. No change in the haggard hulk that stared back at me. Still the same weathered, slack-jawed, maybe a bit stupid, sailor. Pirate wihout an eye-patch. Not a trace of Horatio Nelson, Hornblower, Errol Flynn, or Orlando Bloom... (well, maybe a hint, around the eyes). But no younger. It's a cinch that stuff does not make you smarter.

I grabbed the clipping for another look. Should I get an airplane ticket to... Majorca? But no; I told her I wasn't... do you suppose... could it be possible...would anybody believe this?

#

Capt. Chuck Gnaegy

Three

Pirates in Caribbean History

Blackbeard – Edward Teach – was a huge brigand who tied hemp into his beard and set it afire during battle to strike fear into his prize galleons'crews, in 1713. Armed with two swords, pistols and knives, he cowed even his own crew. When his quarry didn't resist, he'd take their booty and let them sail away. If they put up a fight, he was a raging monster. He captured the French gunship Concorde and renamed her Queen Anne's Revenge, scourge of the American coast and Caribbean. By 1718 he commanded four warships and 300 pirates, capturing 40 vessels, killing hundreds of people. At last, cornered by a fleet of Royal Navy ships at Okracoke Inlet, South Carolina, his body sustained five bullet wounds and 24 sword slashes. The Navy Captain decapitated Blackbeard and hoisted his bloody head to the mainmast, supposedly to show all other Pirates the fate that awaited them, if they continued their wicked, wicked ways. Right or wrong, one must wonder if the examples had any effect. Here, almost 300 years later, following are true stories of modern booty on the High Seas:

The Grass Menagerie:
Bombed in the Bahamas

Run, Chicken Little, It's Raining Money

Two hours before dawn. Suddenly the night was shattered by an unearthly roar as a big twin-engined plane screamed overhead. What? 50 feet off the top of my mast!.

I jumped a yard straight up off my bunk. What the hell? Did this guy think our anchor light was the Riding Rock beacon?

I staggered up on deck, mad as hell, in time to watch the kamikaze bank around for another pass— but he wasn't in trouble, wasn't flying blind. The night sky was clear; with the gibbous moon they write songs about. Then I saw them. Not more than a couple of anchor line lengths away, a dozen sleek go-fast boats were lined up, two by two, in a makeshift runway-guide system, with three red lights, three green, and a series of whites.

But big Jake overhead was not landing out here. Not with 14 feet of water under my keel. So what the skullduggery? The deck-duster thundered overhead again, then I heard a loud "whop" as something smacked the dark water.

Godforbid, I realized, with a gut-wrenching feeling. We are in the middle of a pot drop.

Anchored out, a world away from anything resembling a community, at Riding Rock, southernmost of the Bimini chain of islands. About a million miles from

Miami, the U.S. Coast Guard, or any pattern of organized law. Just me, Girl Friend, and Daughter (mine). This was a supposed peaceful summer idyll on my 40-footer *Payday.* The only excitement planned for today was hauling in a net full of lobsters for lunch and dinner, and winning the world championship of Scrabble, among the three of us.

By now, Girl Friend and Daughter crawled sleepily up on deck. Sleep under this racket... not a chance. I advised them we were watching a real-life modern game of Piratica called *Smuggling,* otherwise known as *Save the Bales.* Silently, we watched as the ghostly bird of prey preened toward its finale. The dropper craft I recognized; a venerable gooney-bird – WWII DC-3 of TV fame. Old, slow, creaky, wings flapping, engines groaning, but able to carry more bales than a fleet of International Harvesters.

After each "whop" a needle-nosed Cigarette sidled out of the "runway" formation, throaty engines burbling, wallowing over to snatch its bale from the black sea. Bizarre, a Grade-B movie starring John Agar. We were an unwitting audience to this dance of the skull and bones. In deathly fascination and silence we saw the DC-3 zoom through its last run, then it rumbled off to the southeast towards Jamaica, where it was rumored the grass grows greener, on its maritime way to Miami. One by one, the free-booters sidled to their salty pick-ups. They roared off, revved to 70+ MPH a few yards beyond the Castle Rock pass beacon.

Then, just as the anchorage was almost clear, Girl Friend grabbed me with enough force to dislocate my shoulder, squealing like a three year old at a birthday bash, "They missed one!"

Sure enough, there was a black, squarish hulk floating less than a hundred yards from *PayDay*. A genuine honest-to-god *square grouper*.

"We've got to pick it up!" Girl Friend yelled.

"Got to? Wait a minute," I said. "I am not about to get into competition with those blood-thirsties. They will kill you for what is in that floating coffin."

"But," she whimpered, like a kindergartner, "they are all gone."

Not true, Most of them had slipped out through the pass between Riding Rock and Castle Rock; two or three were still around, less than a quarter mile away. They appeared to have no interest in us.

"Uh, what would one of those depth charges be worth?" I ventured to Girl Friend.

"Retail," Girl Friend mumbled, "the good stuff goes for about $100 to $500 an oh-zee, an ounce, that is. So it's worth, on average, maybe, uhm, $3,000 a pound. That means a whole bale could sell about eight or ten thousand bucks, wholesale. Say as much as 30 thousand retail." I tried to follow this arithmetic, but at four ayem in the morning I was tired and my brain was not working. And unlike Girl Friend, I could have trouble figuring out the tab at Burger King when they start puffing up all the extras. One thing I did know was old *Payday* was worth about 150 grand as she sat, and I was sure I didn't want her ending up in a government storage depot waiting for auction. I was also sure I didn't want to risk three to seven years in the slammer at this or any age. Most important, not to risk my beloved daughter's future. Not for eight or ten or twenty thousand lousy bucks. "I wouldn't mind a little spending money," I offered, "but I do not relish the idea of being tagged with a whole bale of what we used to call wacky tabacky."

"Nobody gets caught," Girl Friend blurted. "It is the easiest money you can ever make." There was a slight note of disdain in her voice, and I realized with a sinking heart that she was giving me the one challenge no man can ignore. She was calling me yellow.

"Well," I asked Daughter, "What do you think about taking this back to Miami and getting rid of it?" The 'black tuna'— notice how I was picking up the lingo already— was now only 20 yards away and closing fast on our darkened bow.

Daughter was matter-of-fact in her answer... "I know of four or five dealers who would buy it from you tonight."

That was not altogether a surprise. As a modern parent I was aware of some of my baby girl's activities, but blessedly had not been tuned in on this facet of her private life, if there was one. But after all, she was now almost a complete grown up lady, in college, and without a doubt had a brush or two with the seamier side of life. How far she would go with that I could not control from this point on. I could only hope her early training had sunk in, like "Do as I say and not as I do." I'd rather not know all the details.

By now, it seemed as though I was the only one on board who did not know your basic grass dealer who could take an extra supply of salt water soaked pot off your hands. It also seemed that we must now have a quorum of consent for entering the smuggling trade. "Save the bales," I muttered to myself. "Take a pusher home to lunch."

The dark square bobber was nudging its shoulder against the hull now, and I latched on. Heavy. I mean, I have hoisted aboard a few man-sized fish, a five gallon bucket or two of spare fuel, and even an errant crewman who has slopped himself in good Jamaican rum enough to need a boost. This square grouper, however, was the most obstinate damned cargo I ever tried to dredge up from the briny with my bare hands.

Covered in burlap, sewn with one seam across the top, wrapped in a plastic garbage bag, sealed with adhesive tape which is not impervious to salt water. Water-soaked grass is a lot bigger than the hundred pounds it started out with.

Girl friend leaned over the rail and dug her hands into the smelly muck. Gaining on it, we'd heave, clutch, and just as I was sure my hernia operation had been for naught, wrestled it on deck. The fetid odor engulfed us, and a brown rivulet of tobacco juice poured out the scuppers. Shiver me timbers, we are in the wicked trade.

"Those seadogs can smell this garbage a mile away," I said, only slightly less panicked than if I had snatched a sack full of Mafia receipts. Did I hear a motor-boat?

There, off the stern, I saw a big spotlight flash, sweeping the black seas horizon to horizon. Silhouetted against the dim line that separates dark sea from black sky, I could just make them out. Looking for their lost sheep. Three boats, scanning the ebony waters, barely visible as the moon ducked backward into a cloud. But even with their lights out, I saw their filmy wakes. Sidling up closer to us. They knew we were there; my anchor light advertised our presence all night. We could be minutes from a very unsettling discovery.

"We've got to toss this booty back," I panted.

"The hell we do," Girl Friend snapped, wrapping her skinny arms around the giant beanbag like her bed poodle.

"Shut up," I ordered, resuming command of my ship. "We are going to get slaughtered if they find this scurvy cow-pie on board us." Dreadful images – machine guns, bambooed fingernails, hanging by my thumbs – assaulted my mental plane. A boat was closing in, headed for us. No time to argue.

"Go below," I choked. "Get my shotgun over the forward bunk." That shotgun, a recent addition to my modest arsenal, since I have not been blind and deaf to the free publicity Miami and environs has garnered about the dope trade. Loaded with double-ought buckshot, capable of cutting a man in two at close range, it could add a "never miss" reputation to a fading gunslinger. Doc Holiday, or Jeremia Hawke, would be proud. Girl Friend, a quail hunter and crack skeet shot, knew how to handle the short barreled beast. And because I also carried a .357 magnum revolver whenever cruising away from recognized authority, I slid open the drawer at my steering station, and suddenly found the awesome weapon nestling coldly in my trembling hand. This was no drill.

"If they get past me and come into the cabin, do not hesitate," I muttered, my voice a deadly imitation of Clint Eastwood – Jack Nicholson -- Bambi?

Tense, I waited, gripping the big pistol in both hands. What had happened to my summer idyll, I grieved. I brought my daughter on an ocean trip to experience a dose of paradise. Half an hour ago I was anticipating Endless Summer and another day in Eden; nothing more serious than a challenge to my Scrabble championship. Now the night had morphed into Captain Blood, Dracuala threatening to suck out my brains. Suddenly I wished I were back home in the Big Apple. Brooklyn had seldom limned so special. A taste of paradise lost; now seasick in the smuggle jungle.

Sweat on my upper lip dribbled to my mouth with salty fingers. I could hear my own breath, feel the pulse throb in my veins. Two hundred yards away, the big spotlight swung around to center on us, broad side. It hovered there, the boat lit up like neon Broadway. I could hear male voices, but not the words. What? Fire a shot in their direction? Step into the light so they know I know?

Crank the engine and get the hell out of there? Cut the anchor rode? Slowly slink away? Nothing was just right. If I would shoot, they could bring up AK-47s and pulverize us. If I showed myself, they could realize I was the lone male aboard, and charge right in. If I started my engine, no way to outrun those thousand-horse Cigarettes.

I couldn't slink away without more suspicion that it was I who had dipped out their smelly shrimp basket.

I could do nothing. And that is exactly what I did.

The spotlight, in all its sunrise glory, wavered, faded, snapped out. The boat made an abrupt turn, gliding away. The light speared on again, facing another path.

They had decided, I hoped, not to get close enough to be identified, or risk a confrontation with an unknown quantity. Hah, I thought to myself; on a boat this size there could be ten men with machine guns, a rifle grenade, even a missile-launcher. They chugged away, and I felt wildly for a moment a wet spot on my bathing suit; was that warm sweat running down my leg?

"Okay, " I rasped. "They are gone."

The Great Gift of Grass

Girl Friend appeared from below, unperturbed, the brutish shotgun slung on her shoulder.

Like cross bones, a thick box of plastic garbage bags clutched in her hand. She drew a long butcher knife and plopped down on the afterdeck beside the black treasure. "I am glad that showdown is over," she chirped matter-of-factly, Tess Trueheart to her faithful horse, Leadbelly.

"What are you doing now?" I asked.

"This whole bale is too heavy. Got to break it down into bricks," she retorted, all business. "We'll have to get it off the boat in Miami without every Tom, Dick, and dock-walloper knowing we have a guilty secret."

"Whoa. Wait. Just one minute," I said. "I am still not convinced that we ought to be getting a fresh start in the contraband plunder collection. How do we sell this so-called controlled substance, and to whom is the highest bidder? Even before that, how do we get it back to Moon over Miami without the Coast Guard, the U.S. Customs and the Florida Marine Patrol sniffing out we have entered a new freebooting venture?"

"Ha!" Girl Friend snorted. "The Coast Guard is all surrounding Cuba, providing safe passage for illegals and kookoos that Fidel Castro is spewing into American society; and rallying to interdict 60-foot Haitian cargo boats with 300 more pending citizens aboard. Customs is patrolling for speedboats spurting into the Inland Waterway in the middle of the night, full of happy snow-white talcum powder."

Just warming up, she raved on. "The Marine Patrol is least of all interested in a typical family grouping in a nice conservative cruising yacht, motoring across the Gulfstream bringing American money back to the Gold Coast. All we do is trot out the fishing poles and outriggers, wallow back to Miami, then tie up at the dock."

I was stunned by her offhandedness. I would have thought the brush with killer-smugglers would open her eyes to the obvious. We were strictly amateurs and as such would more than likely pull a fatal, stupid goof, then end up slammed for five to ten and out in seven for good behavior. But I knew the female mind does not work that way. And the courts would not treat the female gang-lord the same. Yet, I realized we had not checked into Bahama Customs either, because we arrived after the five o'clock closing time, and it is cheaper to anchor out overnight than to pay overtime charges. So we were technically not ashore in the foreign country, and therefore not required to register with U.S. Customs on coming back. The thought did not occur to me that genuine smugglers don't mess with bothersome formalities.

"Okay, but how, if we get it back there without getting caught, how do we get rid of it, and how soon?" I wanted to know.

"I can call one guy who will take half of it in one bite," Girl Friend said, "and pay us cash on the barrel-head. He will know other guys who will buy all the rest." She was working with a vengeance now, separating the foul-smelling lump from its burlap shroud, until finally it sat there, foreboding, its B.O. strong enough to be scented from there to Miami without crossing the 50-mile Gulfstream.

"Cover it up," I told her. "It stinks." Entire deck was layered with leaves and twigs. Brown iced tea was running down the scuppers. I held a plastic bag as Girl Friend stuffed a fifth of grass inside. Quickly it was tied off, then another and another.

We bagged and tied five separate bundles of pot, altogether. I stowed them in the aft lazarette.

The Methane'll get you if you don't watch out

"See how easy it is," Girl Friend said, a devil's grin on her face; but then a thoughtful look. I knew she was ready to shake me with a poser. "Except," she said, "we cannot leave it in there all sealed up like in a coffin."

"What do you mean?"

"I mean we've got to air it out. This grass, this kind of grass, is hay. Pure and simple. Hay generates heat when it gets wet. And the heat comes from gas. Methane gas."

"So?"

"So methane gas explodes."

"What? What the hell are you talking about?"

"Spontaneous combustion," Girl Friend said. Her thoughtful look had now retrogressed, to Uncle Remus instructing his brood of awe-struck pequeno-ninos. "Hay does it all the time. That's why farmer's barns catch fire. A bale of hay gets wet, and it is sealed up in there without enough oxygen. It makes methane gas."

"Yeah? Then what?"

"Boom."

I stared at her, horror struck. Rolled her eyes.

I muttered an expletive deleted. "Look, we are not going to bring that stuff into the cabin, or spread it on the decks to dry. The grass is going to stay in the bag. A bird in the cage is worth two on the loose."

"Huh-uh."

"The grass is going to stay in the bags. In the hold. Out of sight, out of mind." I had my heels dug in.

"Okay, if you want your boat to explode. Go ahead." She knew she'd win. Used to getting the upper hand by putting her foot down.

I was now between the devil and the deep blue. *PayDay* was the unwilling storeroom of a hundred pounds of contraband, which I was about to — not unwillingly— take responsibility for in return for the recompense, as well as the thrill of adventure. But not willing to risk *PayDay* blown to smithereens. Dodging the U.S. Roughriders was one thing; flirting with impending holocaust another. "You are dead set certain of that? Spontaneous loving combustion?"

Virtue Triumphs in the End

"I lived on a farm twenty years," Girl Friend snapped. "I know about haystacks from first hand experience. Either you air it out, or it goes kablooey."

"That does it," I said, again assuming command as

captain of the ship. "The stuff is going deep six without a jury trial." I moved toward the lazarette.

Girl Friend followed me, yapping like a Jack Russell terrier after a postman's leg. "We can lay it out on the bunks and put down plastic tarps so it don't get everything yucky. We can poke holes in the garbage bags and hang some of it from the radar mast, a little at a time until it all gets dry! We can..."

Too late. My steel trap, too, was slammed.

Quickly I strode to the hatch cover and opened it. The pungent perfume of wet grass, old socks, and messed diapers told me it was indeed not safe and dry down there. I could almost feel the methane gas collecting in little corners, a sly grin on its face, waiting to multiply enough to blow its fuse. Tonight the lazarette, tomorrow the world!

One by one I grasped the slick, plastic, dark green garbage bags and flung them over the stern into the waiting ocean. "The sea giveth and the sea taketh away," I philosophized. But I could see, even in the light of the pale moon, Girl Friend's scowl of outrage and pain. On hands and knees she bent, sniffling, to scrape up enough crumbs for one little joint. Curiously refreshing, it struck me. I knew I was going to pay. She knew it, too.

From then on, I knew our summer idyll was destined not to be all tranquility and spice. I had won the battle; I would lose the war.

But there were days to come. It was not over.

Comes the Denouement...

Four days later I was lounging in a little bar at the foot of Paradise Island bridge, sipping a sweet local concoction called Nassau Royale, and sampling a tasty dish of Coconut shrimp. Girl Friend and Daughter had all but recovered from the ordeal of watching our errant cargo float out to sea. They were on Bay Sreet, Nassau, terrorizing the shopkeepers; buying straw hats and shell bangles.

I was mellow. Pleased with my tropic idyll that now seemed back on track and galloping towards paradise enow. No unpleasant memories of a certain night skulked back to haunt my interlude. On the next stool, a hardbitten yachtsman turned a grizzled face, with a black eye patch. He knew I had just arrived.

"Got any ideas about the mystery?" His name was Bobo and he once-overed me blearily, through his rum-softened eye. He could crew for Edward Teach.

"Probably not," I answered. "Just what is the mystery?"

He unfolded a newspaper with yesterday's date. The headline was bold and black: *"Signs of Damage Deepen Mystery at Sea."*

I read it, hastily. A yacht was found adrift, remote, some distance from our adventure, in the early morning just two days later. Both man and wife... missing. Yacht peppered with pellets and bullet holes. Robbery was not the motive. The electronics were still aboard; the dinghy was riding on its tether, outboard engine still attached. There was speculation; Pirates, Drugs, say the locals who were queried about the case. Pirates, Drugs, say the ham radio operators, whose grapevine tells them everything. Pirates, Drugs, say the police detectives who investigated. The yacht happened on a drug transfer, they all say.

Pirates kidnapped and murdered them.

Bingo. Game over. Exit right this way.

Suddenly I felt a chill. I gingerly told Bobo about that certain night. About our location. About my ultimate decision. "One hundred pounds of Jamaican pot," I said. "Worth eight or ten thousand smackeroos, wholesale, on the open market."

Bobo rocked back in his chair-stool. "Eight thousand," he scoffed. "I only hope your navigation is done by computer, and not by the arithmetic in your head. Good Stuff is now $100 to $500 an oh-zee — that's an ounce— at retail. Average that times sixteen gives you $4,800 a pound."

"Sure," I said, "and maybe $3,000 wholesale. So for a hundred pounds, that — I paused to gasp as it hit me between the eyes— Girlfriend is not perfect by any standard, but never have I known her to err when crisp lettuce was at stake. $3,000 x 100 lbs.... not thirty thousand. "We're talking *three hundred thousand dollars!*"

"And you threw it back," Bobo said.

"Yeah," I said. I was quiet for a long moment. That is a lot of moola. I picked up the newspaper again and read the mystery story one more time. "Yeah," I said at last, " I threw it back." I paused... "But..."

"But they didn't," Bobo said; quickly skipping to the last page.

"Well, no regrets," I said. "Hey, pass me some coconut shrip, okay?"

#

CAPT. CHUCK GNAEGY

Four

Pirates in Caribbean History

Jose' Gaspar, aka Gasparilla, famous for the annual Florida State Fair celebration in Tampa, was not really a Pirate after all. Just a fictional Public Relations stunt dreamed up for a fun theme that could entertain the local population and perhaps draw tourists to the area. It boasted many delights to indulge, including magnificent beaches, sparkling waters, and some of the greatest fishing in the U.S.

Since beginning in 1904, Gasparilla Days include a mock invasion and a parade through the downtown main streets to the marina area, plus arcades, rides, and art shows. The whole affair was patterned after New Orleans'Mardi Gras. The parade ending has mythical Gasparilla leaping off his sinking ship with chains around his neck, vowing never to be captured, while his Mystik Krewe hails the "Last of the Buccaneers." Great fun for revelers, if only make believe .

Read on to find true Pirate tales of today: none funny, but a look into the perils of sea travel, sometimes, in some places.

Real Pirates of the Caribbean

Today They're Not Funny, and They're Still Out There, Lurking

Antigua - Barbuda

These are true stories; however, names have been changed to protect victims from reprisals.

Late afternoon, far offshore over the Atlantic Ocean, the big patrol plane throttled back to drop down over a needle-nosed yacht. I could see it down there; sails bellied, heeled off the wind, its frosty-blue cabin-top and polished mahogany deck giving ready identity. No question – she was *QuayLaMer*, a blue water racing sailboat hijacked, *Pirated*, only yesterday out of Antigua-Barbuda in the British Leeward Islands.

Ironically, Antigua was once, in the 1700s, the HQ of the British Caribbean fleet, purposely built and mobilized to stop Piracy during its most proliferous period. It is today still a popular get-way, with the finest harbor. Princess Margaret honeymooned there.

The Pirate crew had seen us coming. As a guest/observer aboard the U.S. Coast Guard plane I had a bird's-eye view of the operation. The U.S.C.G. radio message was terse, direct:

"*QuayLaMer*, you are ordered to reverse course immediately."

The Pirates quickly came about on another tack, heading toward a darkening squall line. Cocky, certain rough seas and low clouds would shield their getaway; they'd wait for darkness.

The plane circled, dogging the sleek racer, and on another frequency radioed its position to other searchers. Off the yacht's starboard bow the plane dropped a surrender order in a plastic jug. Pinpoint accuracy. The Pirates nosed into the wind, snatched up the bottle, and signaled back derisively with middle fingers. A squall line was closing fast; the plane could not follow forever.

Night fell and the yacht bore ahead, days from land, pointed toward sanctuary in the South Seas. By midnight of the second day, however, more company had arrived. The 95-foot Cutter *Cape Coral* had eased up 300 yards astern, out of normal rifle range, shadowing the yacht. At dawn, the Pirates watched as the Cutter's crew uncovered a deck-mounted 50-caliber machine gun. Closing in, a bullhorn voice boomed across the calm sea.

"Aboard the *QuayLaMer*! You have a choice! Either you give up or we will sink the boat!" It continued, "The owner is on board with us and has given permission to blow you out of the water!"

Defiant, the Pirates revved their engine, bent on escape. "Flip You!" they yelled back. But there was no way they'd outrun the Cutter.

The Commander called once more, "*QuayLaMer*, You have 60 seconds!"

The machinegun chug-chug-chugged a splash of jacketed bullets ahead of the bow.

The message sank in. Three Pirates, two ex-Marines and a former Brit Coast Guardsman finally hove to and raised their hands. Their dream of sailing the boat to

Southeast Asia and returning with a fortune in heroin had gone down the scuppers.

They confessed, gave up its backers in exchange for five-year sentences. Two centuries ago they would have been hanged on the spot. Having committed high-seas Piracy – seizing a vessel by force and kidnapping the crew – they had made more than one mistake. Even though 500 miles at sea, they had dumped the crew overboard but left a small inflatable, with no supplies. In a quirk of fate, the crew was sighted and picked up by a banana freighter next day. It was limping off the sea-lanes with engine trouble.

While stories circulate about Pirates today in Sumatra, the Straits of Malacca, South China Sea, Bangladesh, Nigeria, the Red Sea; the Caribbean is also ripe for daring, lawless men, and women, who live a life of crime. Pirates are not attractive, funny, or entertaining like Johnny Depp.

Peter Blake, a legendary yachtsman who captained the New Zealand sailing crew to win the America's Cup Race in 1995 and 2000, was gunned down aboard his yacht on the Amazon River, murdered by Pirates, just last year. All the swag they got was a few Rolex watches.

In recent years past, some 200 boats have disappeared with little information. Later Piracy has occurred in the Carib, but now most drug shipments arrive in foreign freighters, deeply and cleverly disguised as other merchandise. The yachts which have disappeared left no trace, though a few have been recovered, sans crew. And the Pirates won't talk.

The frequency of attacks and disappearances on the

high seas was evidence enough to provoke a full investigation; the DEA mounted special operational dragnets in the Carib to stop the Pirates, and curtail narcotics smuggling. Those agencies found a definite pattern ... large boats, over 40 feet, worth several hundred thousand dollars, capable of cruising long distances in any weather, and carrying good sized cargoes. That gravitated into mother ships, which serviced small "go-fast" boats, which in turn, could on-load smaller quantities of drugs and outrun Coast Guard pursuit into the Florida Keys, Miami, Tampa. Also to points north off the Carolinas. Those were original Pirate hangouts, where Black Beard was busted.

The Pirated yachts manage to blend in with the hundreds of cruising boats all around the Carib. The Pirate profile, on the other hand, didn't develop any Black Beards or Henry Morgans, even Jean Lafittes. They were mostly clever amateurs; bearded, long-haired, earringed, yes, but they weren't chasing the gold bug. Most would settle for one good haul, as opposed to a lifetime of outlaw Piracy, or so they professed.

One day at a Miami Marina, a sailor docked next door proudly invited me into his sailboat; where one narrow aisle down the center was packed on both sides with odiferous bales. He had automatic weapons, too. I sailed for the Keys that afternoon, close-mouthed, not borrowing trouble. The Caribbean, from Venezuela to Panama and Jamaica, to Miami and the U.S. east coast, became the hottest route for drug traffic since the "French Connection" was severed and the U.S. Customs shut off the tidal wave of marijuana pouring across the Mexican border. But smugglers as well as Pirates have a way of figuring new ways of trafficking.

The evidence left by some smugglers confirms the fears of many yachtsmen about safety at sea, even though modern electronic communications make big differences now. Yacht crews have been murdered, their boats used to haul narcotics, then sunk without a trace.

Colombia:

The yacht *Impromptu*, a sparkling white 42-foot ketch-rigged motor-sailer, rested quietly in the harbor at Cartagena, Colombia among dozens of others of like quality. Nicely turned out, *Impromptu* was an outstanding example of what the yachting fraternity calls "a nice little boat." It had nestled into the colorful harbor for some time while its occupants toured the city of Cartagena, one of the most picturesque in South America. Noted for its coffee, emeralds, its roots from Spanish Conquistadors; also favored for fine quality Peruvian cocaine and Colombian marijuana. Onboard *Impromptu* were its owner, Dan Seybold – once a charter customer of mine – and his good friend from college, Bill Wargel. Seybold's past may provide some clue to what eventually happened with his boat, his friend, and himself. A wealthy man, he was alleged to have been "close to the drug business, perhaps a sometime customer" but also to have associates who were "clean" at the time of his jaunt to Cartagena. Whole truth was perhaps doubtful.

Weighing anchor for a short run north to Panama's San Blas islands, then through the Canal and up the U.S. west coast, Seybold hired two French-speaking crewmen. Jean-Pierre and Denis claimed to be experienced yacht racers who needed passage to California and eventually Canada. They were willing to barter their crew service for the ride. Nothing suspicious there, this happens regularly in yachting circles.

Except that *Impromptu* never arrived in Panama. Months later, after a check had been made by Seybold's uncle in the States, with the San Blas marina, the Coast Guard was alerted that *Impromptu* hadn't shown up. An extensive radio and air search turned up nothing. After three more months the yacht was reported in Jamaica, where marina employees said the young French captain was most charming. Two more months passed, and *Impromptu* was sighted off Dominica, a small, mountainous island half way down the Windward isles in the Carib. Finally, at the urging of Seybold's family, the yacht was stopped in Guadalupe.

Aboard: "Captain" Jean Pierre Motif, and Denis Serge Fennel. Both holding French passports, both with records for smuggling narcotics. Motif was a French Army deserter. They claimed Seybold, being tired of sailing, had gone to Mexico with his friend by railroad. Because of their willingness to crew for months at no wages, the wealthy owner had made them a present of *Impromptu*. They had the title registry.

In the States, Seybold's uncle, shocked but not satisfied with the story, hired a private investigator to dig up the facts. After some time, he reported that he thought Seybold and Wargel had been murdered; the yacht stolen, and was somehow connected to the narcotics trade. The private eye was no Sam Spade, however. Shortly after his report he too, was mysteriously killed. Then the family received a threatening letter from a drug informant in Central America. So afraid, they asked the feds to close the case. Piracy and drug smuggling won out.

Grand Cayman:

A similar Piracy case involved *Mi Peregrine*, a 44-foot trawler, not quite as luxurious as the forerunner, but a comfortable passagemaker nevertheless. It picked up a crew at the Caribbean's Grand Cayman Island, to help its owners ferry it through the Panama Canal to Acapulco, Mexico. After taking on extra rations of food, water, and fuel – enough for months at sea, *Mi Peregrene* left port ... and subsequently disappeared. The crew, six bearded young men from California, are suspected of drug trafficking, but none have been found, and the yacht has never been sighted or identified in any port. Pirates of the Caribbean had struck again.

The idea of Pirates/Smugglers was addressed by drug runners using their own money to buy boats; and that would probably be appropos for the giant cartels operating out of South America and Asia. But the average start-up operation compares favorably to the Pirates of old: That is, why spend your own money when the pickings are so easy. Go out and steal one, so the whole business gets started for free. In one 18-month period, some time back, Coast Guard patrols seized more than 600,000 lbs. marijuana; Street value many millions

The lives of innocent bystanders mean nothing. In one instance, also some time ago, not a fresh case, four young tourists apparently happened on a drug operation involving a mid-range cabin cruiser, in the Florida Keys. They were two young women from New Jersey and two brothers from Maine, found murdered. Each was neatly shot in the head, and their bodies left along the coral encrusted shore. Police assumed they had stumbled upon the landing of a small yacht during transfer of narcotics.

Drug traffic was intense on Puerto Rico. Homicides in San Juan were linked to the drug trade, including Piracy/theft of boats as well.

As a U.S. Commonwealth the Puerto Rican coast is an international boundary of the U.S. Any drugs landed there (also illegal aliens) can be shipped to arrive in Miami markets without U.S. custom checks. A number of boats coming in from Colombia have landed at small island named appropriately Caja de Muertos – Coffin Island. For a time, big shipments unloaded there, trans-shipped in smaller lots to the many tiny coves and inlets along the P.R coast.

A productive ploy used for a time was for boats to drop their cargo at the island, then clear Customs, and return to upload the drugs – cocaine, heroin, hashish – then head for the U.S.

One known drug Pirate/Smuggler was wanted in the high-handed theft of three yachts, including one from Martinique, and two from the Isleta Marina on P.R.'s northeast coast village of Fajardo. Armed and dangerous, carrying several automatic weapons, his photo was shown to a number of people, but he was so fearsome, nobody would name him or point him out. He was nicknamed Black Barteromo, but was never captured.

Another yacht that was suspected of being Pirated by Barteromo was *Cygnet*, a pleasure yacht with a dozen young Americans aboard. Reportedly owned by two

Americans who chartered it for diving expeditions, *Cygnet* headed south in the Carib for Aruba one summer's day, but never arrived. At the time it generated massive air-sea searches covering more than 100,000 sq. miles. Then the Coast Guard began thoroughly checking files of the passengers. They found nine had previous drug records. One young woman had served as crew aboard another yacht, *Ingrid*, in the Virgin Islands before signing on to the dive boat. *Ingrid* was later seized off Carolina, transferring 7 tons of pot onto a fishing vessel.

Digging further, the Coast found that *Cygnet* had questionable documentation, had apparently been Pirated months before, and had been involved in smuggling. With changes in rigging and a new paint job, she had managed to escape capture for many months. Other reports say *Cygnet*, with her new identity in question, was later stripped and burned to the waterline in Colombia. New yachts were easy to come by, for Pirates. I found in talking with Coast Guard officers that, however clumsily, it seemed possible to get away with Piracy for a time, by altering the yacht's nameplate and rigging. But eventually the jig would be up; so Pirates, like most criminals, had to always be on the lookout for new horizons. A number of trawlers had disappeared over time in the Gulf of Mexico in particular, one told me, and a couple had been sighted at different times under new names. Some, we think, had simply been stolen by their crews, he said.

One of the oldest modern tales of Piracy began off Islamorada in the Florida Keys, more than 30 years ago. A charter captain named Angus Boatwright was taking his charter party to Cay Sal Bank, to fish, when he saw a yacht apparently in distress. Since Marine rules require any boat to aid another in trouble, Boatwright veered off and came alongside. The crew of the other boat leveled machine guns and ordered Boatwright to heave to. When he did, they leaped aboard his boat, spraying bullets. Captain Boatwright sank to the deck, killed. The Pirates marooned his charter party on a small spit of uninhabited land in the Bahamas.

After that act of Piracy, they took off for Cuba; a big mistake back then. Though Castro's island has been at odds with the U.S. for half a century, it does not want to be labeled on the world's stage as harboring criminals. Instead of giving sanctuary, the Cubans took the Pirates into custody. They remanded them to Bahamian authorities, who like most seafaring nations (although Nassau was once the world headquarters for hundreds of Pirates) refuse to think lightly of crimes committed on the high seas. The Bahamian courts quickly found the Pirates guilty, and sentenced them to hang. The sentence was swiftly carried out next morning. Facing that kind of hard nosed treatment, most Pirates steer clear of the Yucatan Channel which separates Mexico and the island of Cuba; preferring instead to chance the Windward Passage between Cuba and Hispaniola.

The U.S. Coast Guard takes advantage of this. International jurisdiction says any of the signatories of that convention (on maritime law) can act on Piracy. If a hijacker takes a ship to Havana, they're really tough – reportedly more so than U.S. courts. For a time, in fact, more than 20 Americans from eight different boats remained in Cuban custody for illegal possession of a contraband material within Cuban waters. Over the years, a number of American boats have been apprehended when they strayed into Cuban waters. Most were set free after being found innocent.

For that reason, any time I've captained a yacht down the southern route of the Gulfstream – and that is perhaps 20 voyages – I pay close attention to the International borderline, and stay at least 15 miles offshore. My boats have been shadowed, sometimes all night, by the Cuban Coast Guard, but have never been stopped for survey. Last year I captained a 41-foot sailing catamaran to Isla Mujeres off the north Yucatan coast, shadowed all night by a Cuban gunboat. It stayed 1,000 yards back, but in plain sight, until we broke contact next morning, a few miles from our destination. That's not always the case – or the luck – with all charter captains.

The yacht *Spoon Bread*, a 38-ft. charter sport fisherman out of Key West, was contracted by a young couple and their small daughter for a day of sight-seeing and shell collecting at Fort Jefferson National Monument, in the Dry Tortugas, some 70 miles west of Key West. They'd perhaps stop at Boca Grande Key or the Marquesas, or Loggerhead Key. When they showed up, however, the group included another man, brother of the customer. Thirty miles from port, near the Dry Tortugas, while its captain readied the anchor, both men smoked marijuana joints. Then the supposed brother pulled a 9mm Luger and leveled it at the captain.

"You're gonna take us to Havana," he said. His glazed eyes showed the effects of the pot smoking, and he was definitely not in the mood for argument. Havana is less than 90 miles from the U.S. and the trip was un-eventful.

Arriving in Havana Harbor, however, the situation changed. Havana police quickly assessed the act of Piracy; they took the man, his wife, brother, and 10 year-old daughter straight to jail. They refueled *Spoon Bread* and released it for return to Key West. The captain never heard what happened to them. This time the Pirate lost.

In another case of Piracy, the good-luck-bad-luck equation saved an owner's life. The 40-ft. motor-sailer *PintaMia* was enroute from Progresso, Mexico to St. Barths in the Carib, then eventually Tampa, Florida. Its American owner, with his good friend and mate, had hired a pick-up crew who claimed they wanted to return to the States. They called themselves Shakh Abdal-ziz, and Abdul Abdul-Aziz, but were actually 42 year-old Horace Wilson and his 18-year-old son, Kevin Alton. Midway across the Gulf of Mexico Wilson, alias Aziz, drew a pistol and told the owner to change course for Brazil.

The excitement of entering Piracy, however, turned out to be too heavy for Wilson/Aziz. As the boat turned to the heading he ordered, he suffered a heart attack.

The yacht owner immediately radioed the Coast Guard and Wilson was evacuated by helicopter to New Orleans. Later he was transferred to FBI custody on a charge of grand theft, Piracy. Sometimes the Pirates can't handle the responsibility.

Some other boat owners have not fared so well. The 52-ft. *Idono*, an Outer Reefs trawler type was char-tered by two couples for a 10-day cruise off St. Lucia, deep in the Caribbean. Famous for its twin volcanoes, the Pitons, with black sand beaches and boasting a drive-in volcano, it is a stellar destination, with some of the finest harbors in the West Indies. Inexperienced seamen, the charterers hired two local men as crew and embarked on their holiday. When they failed to return, the charter company called for a search. The hulk of *Idono* was 200 miles away, burned and sunk. There was no trace of passengers or crew. It was assumed by authorities that Piracy ended in tragedy for that charter.

In spring, the luxuriously outfitted *Saba Sabbath*, a 54-ft. motoryacht, stopped at Nassau, took on supplies, and left for a leisurely cruise through Bahamian waters, headed for Turks & Caicos, and Dominican Republic. Aboard were several New Jersey real-estate developers, apparently looking for island properties to build on. Though not highly experienced seamen, their boat had every conceivable piece of equipment and gadget to make cruising easy. That included radar, auto-pilot, radios and beacons, GPS, single side-band, sat-nav, etc. A month after leaving Nassau it was reported missing, by the company-owners who had heard nothing in that time. The Coast Guard and Bahamas Basra crisscrossed the area for 22 days with ships, planes, and radio signals but found no trace. Later, according to a tip from Lloyds of London, Jamaican authorities had a report of a yacht answering the description of *Saba Sabbath* in Port Royal, for an overnight stop. A crewman had told marina employees they were headed for Aruba, in the Netherland Antilles, west of Venezuela. The report said they expected the yacht had fallen prey to Pirates. It was never located.

A final example, though there is an endless list in Coast Guard files, is the story of *Como Si*, a 65-ft. liveaboard sailing yacht owned by a retired oil man, Ory Mayhue and his wife Bonnie, from Galveston, Texas. They planned to island-hop throughout the Carib, then float through the Panama Canal and up the coast to their second home in Puerto Vallarta, Mexico. The wealthy Mayhew was reported to have $30,000 in traveler's cheques aboard the $1,000,000 yacht. A crack shot, he was also well armed, with a registered shotgun, deer rifle, and a .357 magnum revolver.

After spending the weekend in Corinto, Nicaragua, *Como Si* was never seen again. Speculation, as much as could be figured, was Piracy, and drug traffickers.

To combat the smuggling of drugs and ancillary crime of Piracy, the Drug Enforcement Administration, Coast Guard, and Customs have tried many drives.

The first was "Operation Dragnet" many years ago. It employed 300 narcs, 29 boats and five planes spread out from Ft. Lauderdale. Little was found from that plan.

Later "Operation Buccaneer" was pointed at stopping the flow of ganja – hashish from Jamaica. It stopped a dozen planes and boats, plus 99 Pirates/Smugglers, and allowed Coast Guard cutters to fly a "Cannabis Flag" when they made a catch. But little progress was made in stopping the flow. Even after a year of catching 52,000 lbs. of marijuana and more than 6,000 lbs. of hash, it was the proverbial drop in the bucket. In one catch, the Marine Patrol confiscated 17,000 lbs. of marijuana off Miami, while inspecting a 65-ft. fishing vessel. Two crewmen jumped overboard; were never found. The skipper was thrown in jail. Three days later, a Colombian shrimp boat was seized 46 miles off Ft. Lauderdale, bearing 25,000 lbs. of pot, worth perhaps $16,000,000 wholesale. But Piracy exists in many ports, and while not thriving, still has aficionados who would rather try crime than work for a living.

That wouldn't save Norman Finkbine, who lived aboard his 45-ft. sloop at Red Hook in St.Thomas, U.S. Virgin Islands. His sloop, *Hedonism*, was boarded one night at gunpoint by two drug addicts, a true act of Piracy. Once at sea they killed him, dumped his body overboard, and took the sailboat to Tortola, in the British Virgin Islands. They forged ownership papers and sold the yacht for $75,000. Arrested later on drug charges, one Pirate, in hopes of amnesty, gushed out the whole story and pled guilty to a lesser charge. His accomplice was convicted of murder. Those are some of the stories we know about. There are many more happening yesterday, today and tomorrow we have yet to see. A few young and determined Pirates can take possession of an unsuspecting yacht, just as felons can rob a jewelry store, or steal a new car. But like the cities, there are thousands of people who will never be involved as victims or perpetrators. In a few cases, as one Coast Guard Captain told me, the odds are with the Pirates.

It pays to be knowledgeable; and be prepared.

#

Five

Pirates in Caribbean History

Pirate Roche Braziliano was the original Rocky, both in name and actions. A rare, successfu Dutch Pirate, he operated out of Port Royal, Jamaica. That was the buccaneer stronghold for many years, until an earthquake doomed the legendary city, plunging it to the ocean's bottom. Rocky sailed his Pirate barque around Campeche, Mexico, preying on ships out of Havana loaded with treasure. He'd retreat to Port Royal to disport the roaring, wicked life. Captured, he was sent to prison, but managed to have a letter delivered to the Governor threatening his Pirates would burn the city unless he was sent back to Spain. He was, but immediately returned to ravage rich Campeche ships. Rocky remained one of the most bloodthirsty Pirates in the Caribbean.

Amazon, The River Gold

Wild Things, Where the Prey is

You

I knew they were there, all around us.

Piranha.

Swarming Pirate fish of the Amazon. Armed not with cutlass or cannon, but teeth; their flags of red, black and gold, on mottled white, emulate the true colors of those rapacious wolves of the sea.

I could see faint swirls as their blood-red bodies twitched just below the muddy surface, ready to reduce a whole steer – or a man – to a million olive-sized mouthfuls.

Then Beder, my Indian guide, rolled his dark eyes toward the center of the brown river. In his second tooth a small gold inlay glinted in the sunlight, giving him a deadly, mischievous grin. His bare, brown arms and legs showed long, spidery scars that might have come from a series of knife fights. I wondered about his past adventures, and what he might demand of me, in precarious jungle exploits, challenges, or just playing his game.

"Okay," he murmured softly in his sly, Indian rasp, "We go in now. Step down."

Slowly, inch by inch, I shadowed him into the murky water.

The Amazon, biggest river in the world, an impenetrable body of tumultuous green shot through with milk chocolate ribbons. A river swelling with floods, bursting every year out of its normal boundaries, miles wide and deep as a four-story building. A river with raucous clouds of birds, monkeys, peccaries, jaguars and wildlife that flourish in its nearly 4,000-mile serpentine jungle course to the sea. Bounded by Indian tribes, native river villages, nomads, thatched huts and concrete cities. Soaring trees that rival California's giant sequoias; its forest canopy so dense it blocks out the sun on half a continent.

I had sailed my 54' steel motorsailer to Trinidad for interior refitting by expert mahogany wood carpenters; then I had an offer to deliver a yacht to Belem, on the coast of Brazil. I could not resist experiencing the magnificent and haunting Amazon.

A river of steaming jungle heat, pouring rain, bounty, deprivation. Of change, unwillingness to change, of the strange and the wonderful, the pestilent and promising.

The mighty Amazon has it all. Indians named it, reverently, "The River Gold."

Earlier in the morning I had fished right here, hauling in dozens of the piranha on hook and line, avoiding those razor-sharp dentures that gape open even in death. They were like a sunfish or bluegill, tasty and firm.

Now I was offering these ravenous, hand-size predators the same   bargain, as the root beer-brown and green-striped river crept   around my knees. A chill ran up my spine as I felt something small bump my calf.

My excursion had brought me to the great river at its headwaters, via a jungle steamer. Three decks with iron grillwork, it was quite simiar to a New Orleans-style gambling packet. But no Pirate Jean LaFitte. *Rio Amazonas* was quite large for a river boat, at 146 feet, but at peak, carried dozens of passengers.

While I would normally prefer a dugout canoe for the backwaters – and I had a chance for this later – this steamer was geared for four-to seven-day adventure cruises at the jungled beginnings of the Amazon. But on this trip I was its lone passenger, boarding after a scheduled maintenance stop at Manaus. It was a way to explore this magnificent river in relative comfort (even air conditioning), and write my own ticket on just how formidably I wanted to explore.

As a "mother ship" *Rio Amazonas* carried its own shore boats for daily excursions into the deep forest inlets and streams. A larger, all-steel version of the classic riverboat, it boasts 21 private passenger cabins, all on the upper decks. Each private cabin offers all amenities, with large windows and upper deck bathrooms as well. The main dining room provides buffet style meals, plus a well-stocked ship's bar. Since I was the only passenger, I opted to sleep on deck, in a hammock. Night in the jungle river can be an experience in itself, but it was not yet mosquito season. The zooming flights of orange-brown, flapping fox-bats, with their three-foot wing spans, ignored me.

One part of the river boat's tour winds up the river to Peru's *La Selva de los Espejos*, a national reserve named "jungle of mirrors." Its four-day transit stops at jungle towns, native villages, and the confluence of the Maranon and Ucayali rivers, to the Pacaya-Samiria National Reserve. Birders are treated to intimate close-ups of the oriole blackbird, purple gallinule, horned screamers, jacarandas, yellow-headed caracara, as well as a possible glimpse of the predatory, rare, harpy eagle.

Its seven-day, 325 mile Rio Amazonas cruise starts, actually, from Lima, Peru, where, at the end, I overnighted at the suburban Hotel Miraflores. Coming in, a morning flight to Iquitos – Peru's northern industrial hub – quickly takes boarders from the urban jungle to the tangled rainforest on the banks of the great river, where they board the spacious river boat.

My adventure took in a city jaunt of Iquitos, north on the Colombian border – for some reason a metropolitan area much more modern than I expected. There are no roads from Lima; you travel by boat or air to the jungle city. It sports a smattering of tall buildings, banks, offices, even though on some streets I encountered half-naked, nose-boned natives.

The riverside outdoor market offers everything from fresh-caught fish to bows and arrows, even linens.

At Iquitos, ocean-going freighters load and deliver goods, 2,400 miles from the Atlantic, past a floating village at the outskirts where perhaps 5,000 people live in houseboats; then on to a junction of the Tahuayo river and its confluence with the Huisi river, to the Tambo

Tahuayo campsite.

Less than a mile away, deep in the jungle, wild parrots and myriad songbirds create a raucous melody overhead, though barely visible through the dense rainforest. I slept that night at a camp on shore, in a tiny, round-thatched jungle hut. Spiders crawling in the crisscrossed weaving overhead, with one lone candle to cast their spectral shadows larger than life. Tarantulas? Perhaps. A moody, eerily fascinating night.

Most of the second day I spent hiking to *Father Cocha Lake* to drink in the splendid varieties of wildlife, from grunting peccary piglets to soaring blue and yellow macaws. The third day was an excursion to *Charo Lake* to see fresh-water dolphins, and fish for peacock bass, black piranha, corvina or the Zungaro tigre. Bird watching is unavoidable; with more than 1,500 species in the Amazon, many not found in any other part of the world, they make their mark. I reveled in the overnight campout.

The fourth day included short side trips to native villages. Blanco and chorro monkeys whip overhead, or dip down to grab bananas or mango fruit out of your hand, from any of a dozen choices of tropical goodies the ship supplies. In the river, magical pink-white dolphins, 6 to 8 feet long, roll in the deep currents a hundred miles from the sea. A different species from the bottle-nose dolphins, these have longer snouts and seem to be more slender. They are still the happy, playful sea jokers.

In rainy season the river changes from a half-mile wide, 30 foot-deep stream to perhaps twice that, in wild rushing torrents and whirlpools. Native groups have two different riverside houses, one below for dry season, and one built up high on stilts for the rainy season.

All of this I had marveled at, on my trip here. And now, I was tempting the fates as I waded, chest deep, among the circling piranha. What was that, something small, hand-size, bumping against my leg? I feared I would never get out alive. Dreading the attack, I froze.

Then Beder turned to me and smiled. His tooth glinting. "I tell-ed you it's okay," he grinned. "Piranha don' eat people;" thus blowing a hole in some of my most horrifying memories of Hollywood flicks.

He pointed across the short inlet where a group of young children splashed, screeching happily. "See them? They swim there every day." So much for Tarzan flicks.

But I was also told of other hazards lurking, some a man couldn't see. While malaria is not as rife as it once was, it's a good precaution to visit the local health agency for the latest advisories, plus the nearest drug store. Most important, it's not a good idea to swim unprotected in the Amazon. And do not, ever, take a leak while swimming in the rivers. Beder told me of a curious micro-sized catfish that likes to seek out humans, swim up the urine flow into the urinary canal, and attach itself inside the urethra, where it grows to golfball size. It can be removed only surgically – not a happy prospect. For that reason my legs seemed to grow ever longer the deeper I went into that little bay.

Then after a short swim, I was on dry land and ready to visit a native village.

"Don't call them Indians," Beder prompted. "These

are native river people. They would feel insulted. They have climbed well out of the primitiveness of Indian tribes."

Indeed they have. Most villages, however small, have electric power, and education is compulsory in Peru. All but the most backwoods people are literate, many bi-or- trilingual, speaking the native Quechua as well as Spanish and English. Beder, who grew up in the jungle, is fluent in all three, plus Italian and Portuguese. He declined to confide his past, but I sensed it had some rugged chapters.

Of course, there are still native, primitive Indian tribes all along the Amazon, and probably headhunters – Jivaros – somewhat deeper in the jungles, as well.

During my last few days there, I visited with the Yaguar tribe and learned to shoot a six-foot blow-gun well enough to hit a target at 30 yards. They were impressed.

So was I.

Later, I saw the Bora tribespeople delight in their "Dance of the Anaconda," where men, women and children weave in and out in a happy, simple pattern to the shouts and cries of the participants. They like to grab visitors' hands and lead them into the skipping dance. I didn't try to deny the laughing little girl-cherub who pulled me into the Anaconda's writhing pattern; it was such a happy experience. She must have been all of six years old, happy-go-lucky, giggling like little girls everywhere. That fleeting partnership was a voyage I'll always remember.

And of course they have learned that Yankees like

to buy souvenirs.

I couldn't resist a decorated version of the blow-gun for myself, with slender, foot-long darts, and a dart sharpener made from piranah teeth.

But I was warned later to remove the decorative feathers, which may have been dyed in bright colors, but could have come from an endangered species of macaw. If so, it would be confiscated by U.S. Customs. Shorn, it would pass with ease. And I would always have a keep-sake, to remember the mysterious world of the Amazon into which I'd wandered.

I cherish it still.

#

Capt. Chuck Gnaegy

Six

Pirates in Caribbean History

Captain Sam Bellamy, in 1715, convinced an affluent friend that he was a treasure hunter. Bankrolled with a ship to bring back sunken gold and rare gems, he found nothing, but simply couldn't return to Massachusets enpty handed. He hoisted the Skull & Crossbones, and in the space of a year had plundered 50 galleons. Off Cuba, he seized the slave galley Whydah, but on the way back to the Northeast, he ran afoul of a hurricane with 40-foot waves. Whydah was capsized, blown ashore and broken in two. 140 men were killed, including an 11 year-old pirate, John King. The wreck was located in 1984; its booty created the Whydah Center in Cape Cod, with 200,000 artifacts.

Hot Tuna: 101

A College Kid's First Taste of Sea

This was nothing like they promised me. I was green faced, white knuckled, stomach upside down and backward like I had overdosed on liver pizza. Cold terror was crawling up my backbone and warm fear was running down my legs. The sea was lumping into Colorado Rockies, and the wind's howl was quadrophonic heavy metal rock. On top of that, Harley Goosbladder was screaming in my ear to go backwards.

"Back her down! Backer down! *Backer down*! I slammed it in reverse. The boat mushed backward, playing Riddley turtle covering up eggs on late-night Jacques Cousteau. And overhead, a wave that could crush New York City hovered, flicking giant squid arms, tossing whipped cream chunks of spindrift. Soon I was standing in cold sea water up to my peaches. Harley wanted his fish.

"I got to have this tuna! Backerdown!

His pole U-turned, bobbing jungle rhythms between his feet jammed against the railHis line was singing hot soprano and his reel smoked, white-hot. He wanted to cool it.

"Get some water on this reel! And back her down!"

Was this a death wish, or what? This   grandaddy of all fishes,   one thousand pounds of loving tuna fish, he yelled, could honk us to the sea floor one thousand feet of Gulfstream deep. The incredible hulk of waves was poised in the sky, about to dump its entrails on top of us, and I feared ol' Gooz was gonna get his water, soon enough.

I hugged the wheel and asked forgiveness for all my sins. Was this spring break, or what?

"Spring break" is when the college truants get back at winter. Me, I ankled it out from ol' Pottstown State as sunshine beckoned; come down and froth up the rites of spring in Ft. Liquordale, where the girls are. Pull some rays. Topless daze. Tropic highs. Sunayabuns.

Rich kids fly Amurcan. Middle class kids take a Greyhound. I hitch-hike. That's how I hooked up with Harley Goosbladder. Riding my thumb down the Skyline highway, shivering in the morning haze, wondering why spring on the Atlantic is no warmer than Goose Bay. Along came this van, a huge plastic jelly doughnut on top, towing a big boat.

On the side, red paint shouted, *Goosbladder's Krystal Kreme Donuts – the Sinker Kids Love to Dunk.*

With Goose Bay was running through my head, I decided he was my man. I sank down on the roadway, raised my hands in prayer. That gets them every time. On his way to Florida in a nice warm truck towing his own boat. The independent businessman these days is rich beyond my wildest dreams.

A college kid, 18, on my way to the promised land of sunshine where the girls are, couple of bucks in pocket, grin on my face. Largest body of water I had seen was Lake Piscatsoh, which you can't see across either. Harley Goosbladder needs a crew, to the Bahayma Islands, to catch a 1,000 lb. tuna fish, what could I say? Okay.

Big, good natured guy with squinty eyes like Stan Laurel, surprised eyebrows, stickup hair; big barrel chest and jelly do-nut belly over his belt. He slapped me on the back with a meaty hand. He liked slapping people on the back and yelling in their ear.

"Call me Gooz!" He shouted. "Captain Gooz!"

Can all his friends, I wondered, be victims of defective hearing aids, or is this what it does to you, getting up at three ayem every morning to dunk jelly doughnuts in hot grease.

"Hot tuna!" he boomed. "In those Bahayma Islands there, they have one thousand pound loving tuna fish! And I am catching one! I give you the college course, fishing skill one-oh-one!"

"Can you do this? I never saw a tuna fish that big. Only those little ones in a can."

"Ha! Can I catch one? I almost win the Darmstadt Open Muskie Tournament! Those things, too, get big you know. With teeth!"

"You *almost* won?"

"Ha! This Jojo Warbucks, he brings in this seven-pounder. My fish is bigger, but somebody cuts it open and its belly's full of buckshot. Sabotage! I was disqualified, and Jojo Warbucks wins it!"

"Gee. So he got the prize."

"Yeah. He win the bowling meet, too. I'm second. He's my brudder-in-law, I cannot accuse him of making more exes than there are. But now I got him!"

"Bad luck, it sounds like to me," I sympathized.

"Ha! If there is one thing ol' Gooz has got, it is the gift of good luck. Good luck Gooz! That's me. Hey! Know something? Ol' Gooz can be good as Heimingway, or Isaac Walcott, even Jonah, greatest fishermen of all time. Yeah. One thousand loving pounds of tuna fish!"

If I began to learn anything about Harley Goosbladder in a very few minutes, it was that he did not mind talking about himself, and I also suspected he was a driven man. Gooz rapping a mile a minute about his doughnuts, his bowling league, his lodge - the Moose. Through it all, I began to fathom that ol' Gooz has to bring home a winner; to save face over Jojo Warbucks, who always beat him out, in everything.

Nice boat. I asked, "Had it a long time?"

"Ha! Not mine. Alvin Applebrot's! My boat, it sinks in Lake Muckwinango when the drain plug accidentally comes out. We swam to da bank, my wife and me, floating on the beer cooler. She's mad as hell! Wouldn't even come on this trip."

Gooz is always making somebody mad as hell, I guessed. I told him I don't know anything about boats, or engines.

"Ha! Boats, and engines, piece a cake!"

"And fish. I don't know anything about one thousand pound tuna fish."

"Thousand pounds of tuna fish. Piece a cake!"

"Wow. The Bahama Islands. Bimini. Nassau."

"Yeah! Crank the engine! Drop the lines! Piece a cake! Ol' Gooz gives you the college course in fishing!

And that study course is Hot tuna! One-oh-one!"

Lady Luck, however, was lying in wait. No sooner had we cast off from Ft. Liquordale I saw the weather was not among the best. This humongous black cloud, a green center, chasing us for hours, and the deep blue Gulfstream water turned black and gray. Waves looked more like West Virginia than a salt water pond. Tops frothing at the mouth. The sea was mad as hell.

Clouds gaining, rain started pouring down, the boat corking up one side and down the other, playing greased pig in a rain barrel. Big hard raindrops splattering on the windshield like #4 goose shot, and wind shrieking grand opera. I never saw the like on Piscatoh Lake.

Goosbladder was, however, not a scaredy cat. He was yelling his head off, singing some opera song, I figured, German, Ride of the Valkyrie, I think.

Saw me watching, roared laughing. "Hey, da whole family sings!" he yelled. "I got a mudder-in-law can take out all the crystal in Hefflefinger's German restaurant, a Rathskellar! Hey, you think dem Bahaymas like Opera?"

"Maybe, But they only speak English, I think." He couldn't hear me. I couldn't make him out, either, this wind was wolf howls, or grand opera, or a chorus of 1,000 Canadian geese. The VHF radio beeped. I could barely make that out, too, but between the bursts of gravel I felt old Lady Luck was about to take her shot. Something about schools of fish. Two guys shouting back and forth.

Goosbladder Stuck his mouth right up to my ear and yelled, "You hear what he say? Tuna! Entire loving schools of giant loving tuna fish!"

Fire lit his eyes like a vicious dog. The thing he was driven by, coming to pass.

My mind was not on fish. For one thing I was now hanging on by my fingernails and trying to steer the boat, trying not to look at anything except the compass, with my knees wedged against the firewall, and it was spinning from "SE" to "E" every time a boomer slammed into us. Gooz decided to let me drive because, he said, he gets seasick when he has to spin the wheel. As if I was not swallowing my tongue on every breath. Belching scrambled eggs.

But he was far from green like me. He was suddenly buns-up in the fantail locker, shouting something I couldn't hear, and dumping gear on deck by the armload.

As I turned around to watch, the deck was littered with two stiff boat rods, reels, an oaken bucket with some obvious past, a fish-skinning board with a dried pickerel still stuck in the clamp, a mop with a broken handle, a rubber boot, and half a carton of old buttermilk. Then he hauled out a tackle box; broke it open, spewed out its innards, and all of it sliding back and forth in a big jumble. We were wallowing up the edge of a wave that I didn't think was gonna end, then crashing back down sideways. Gooz was not done yet.

He dragged the last thing out, a reel half as big as a gallon bucket, with wire line thick enough to lift the entire boat, and a rod that would have made a good broomstick if they left the eyes off. But closer, I saw it was a device they use to haul up the boat on a trailer; not fishing gear at all. I yelled this intelligence to Gooz. It didn't faze him.

"If you hunt a bear you got to take a blunderbuss!" He screamed. "You got to take a rod to choke a horse! A big kahoona!" The boat lurched suddenly, and he flopped on his jelly doughnut belly into the pile of Stuff. He slid back and forth with it, getting greener by the second, roller-coaster riding, sloshing up and down in gear and foaming water. I turned away, glued to the compass. If he was starting a demonstration in creative omelet mixery in the middle of the deck I didn't want to be involved.

For too long to count, I held my breath and wished myself body and soul back to the serene and solid ivy covered halls of Pottstown State University School of Veterinary Medicine, just to poke at earthworms, basic things like that, dissect cat's livers, slice up frog's eyes, read about the 38 miles of through-way in a bull elephant's bowel. But Pottstown State is stuck on winter, with snow as deep as an elephant's bongo button. And I did not care if cows and camels have two stomachs. On *Spring Break*; playing *Isaac Waltheim*. I strained to bring my head and body back, worried needlessly. Gooz, all smiles, struggled out brandishing a giant killer. Feet kicking, his belly free of the hatch.

"I got the gear!" But even upside down, I could see his eyes were glittery.

"You are certain dead nuts that is a tuna?"

"Ha! Lots of tunas. you hear the radio report! A loving entire school of tuna fishes!" A driven man.

"But," I pled, "I'll bet lots of guys can fish all through their whole lives without finding one blessed tuna fish."

"It's Goosbladder luck! I tell you! Giant loving

charlie tuna fish! And I got it! Goosbladder skill!"

I gaped wildly around at the steepening seas. "The ocean is pretty rough to start fishing. And getting rougher."

"Ha! Piece of cake!" Jack London on a trail of blood and gore; of Canada moose and White Fang.

"I don't know about this," I offered, steering off to keep from smacking a boomer.

"I know!" he yelled. Tarzan with a crocodile.

Grimly, I clutched the wheel, which was getting flimsier in my hands by the minute, as I watched a man stepping into the lion's cage, and dragging me behind.

Eyes rolling , he hauled himself up and out of the mess, wiping froth off his chin. His hair standing on end, like lightning rods. Waving the monster fishing contraption, pointing at something in the water. I strained to make it out between the lumps and rolling and the spray flying off the tops of giant waves. It was something big— maybe a boat upside down I thought— but then it was gone. Then I heard Gooz yelling, into the wolfhowl of the wind. A Neanderthal calling up his voodoo cards.

"Toooo-ooo-naaa! Owooo-naa! Too-naa tooo-nnn-aaa. Hot toonaa. Tuna! Tuna tuna tuna. Toonaa!"

Something out there, for sure, off our starboard quarter. If a tuna it was a big one. As Gooz waved me on, I veered the helm over to get in front of it. I couldn't even see it any more, but he was waving his arms and fumbling with the rod and reel. He rummaged in the up-ended tackle box and pulled out a hook big enough to snag the QE II. It was not a hook at all, I thought, but a flying-gaff with an eye in it, thick as my thumb and long

as a forearm, with a bight the size of a stirrup. Screaming Valkyrie again, Gooz was tying on a whole eight
pound mullet, which I expected he planned to make cut
bait out of for four days. I yelled at him but he was singing "Battle Hymn of the Republic, and the light in his
eyes glowed fit to be Don Juan in Hell. He was Horatio
Nelson shooting up the Spanish fleet. Mindless of the
soaring waves and screaming winds.

"Hey Gooz" I pled, "you are dead set certain that
is a tuna fish? It's more like a Polaris submarine."

"It is a giant loving one thousand pound tuna charlie
fish!" he hollered. "Maybe a world record charlie tuna!
And it is all mine! Tuna you belong to meee!" He ought
to be committed. I was getting desperate.

"Hey Gooz, lots of things come in extra large, you
know. Ocean liners, submarines, bathyscapes. Old oil
tanks. Could be one of those rocket casings from Cape
Canaveral, even. Huh? You know? Or giant squid. I see
them in the old flicks. They eat boats."

"Ain't no giant squid out here! This is one half a
ton of tuna! where in the wonder loving place you think
we are at? Hollywood?"

"The Bermuda triangle! What are we gonna do with
one thousand pounds of tuna fish? I cannot hardly eat
one whole can."

He was rushing us headlong into self-destruct.
Pumped himself with all the rhetoric and positive mental attitudes. He was ready to challenge the King of Neptune himself.

He waved me aside and let the rigged mullet drift
back into the roiling sea. In seconds it was swallowed

up in foam as the black-grey mountains rushed to lift us and chase across our stern. The frigid finger of fate was creeping up my spinal column and for the umpteenth rerun I retreated in my head for warm and steady Pottstown halls of ivy. Then, in a flash, Goosbladder jolted me out of that.

"Strike!" he was yelling. "Strike! A bite! I got it! Igotit Igotit!"

I jerked my head around to watch. There was indeed something in the water back there, and it was on the end of his line. It was burning line off so fast the sprocket was a blur. So fast I heard its whine above the screeching wind. I read once about how salt water fish are so strong, if hooked up tail to tail with fresh water fish the same size, they'd pull the F/F all over the ocean backward. If that is true, it is happening to us and this charlie tuna. Suddenly in full reverse. Boiling backward into waves the like of which could bury the Chicago water tower.

Goosbladder's wire line singing coloratura, so twangy it could call up coyotes. But strong enough to waltz us backward up the downstairs. Alvin Apfelbrot's boat without a handbrake; rolling sixty in reverse. A wall of water lumping up behind us like we had dug our feet into the rug and Daddy was taking us to bed. But Gooz had found his niche.

He'd got his death wish, and we were there. He was exploding with teeth-clenched obscenities, grunting, screaming. Captain Ahab with the full iron in. Tightening the drag on his monster reel. Jerking back his rod into a U-turn, feet braced against the rail with his knees buckled against his chest, tongue lolling out and gagging with the strain.His quarry was not to be cowed. It was leaving on a journey to the center of the earth, to the bottom of the Gulfstream trench, 2,500 feet down, and at its current rate of descent, two minutes to the end. A puff of blue-white smoke was peeling off the screaming reel and instantly dissolving in the wind. He was on fire. The stern was humping up and down. He started to yell.

Was this a fictitious dream? My face was green, my knuckles white, and I was hanging on the wheel with a death grip. My stomach was upside down and backward and a taste of liver pizza overdose was in my throat. Cold terror was crawling up my back-bone and warm fear was running down my legs. The sea was lumping into Colorado Rockies, and the wind was howling quadrophonic heavy metal rock. On top of that, Harley Goosbladder was screaming in my face. He wanted to go faster backwards.

"Back! Her! down! Back-her-down! *Backerdown*!"

I slammed it in reverse. It started huffing backwards into our stern wave and sea water was dumping over the transom. That's when I saw it, this incredible hulk of wavedom, flicking giant squid tentacles, playing tag with the sky above our heads.

"Water!" Gooz is screaming. "Puleeez get some loving water on this reel!"

He had come to the end of his wire. The giant tuna charlie has found the going easy to the last strand. The boat was humping up and down to drown itself stern first in ocean water. Then I saw salvation, hanging right there before me on the bulkhead. A fire-axe! I snatched it loose and dropped the wheel to charge back to Gooz, bent on chopping that line in two and saving our lives.

The wave, however, had different plans. It shoved us side-ways, picking up our stern. The poor boat was trying, too, to save itself, hunkered down on its side in the trough. We were all an hour late and a dollar short, I realized with horror. This thing curled above us, hovering, grinning from on high sucking out a hole in front for us to drop into. Goosbladder was about to get his water alright. I dropped the axe and got out of there.

I dove for the cabin as the noise of Columbia blasting off our deck was just beginning. Then everything turned to dark green as the rumble of the First Infantry double-timed on top our heads and the Budweiser Percherons galloped madly after. I could not think of Goosbladder, or giant loving tuna fish, or if the dawn comes up like thunder in the morning, because at this precise moment in history I was never sure there would be one, or any, of the above. I sucked in my breath and held it until I was green as the liquid skies that blubbered above us, and at last the cabin overhead was bursting out from under that trembling twenty-mule team. I gasped for breath and staggered back to the helm.

Goosbladder, to my never-ending shock was sitting out there, still strapped in the fighting chair. But something was drastically different about that chair. It was no longer sitting up on its pedestal; it was flush with the deck. I groped hand-over-hand back there, to see the three-inch cylinder driven through the deck, and Harley was sitting now at level with the tuna door. But alive. His line still tight and twanging. Not singing, but his eyes rolled slowly at me and he mouthed into the howling wind, "No Ceegar."

I staggered around the deck, surveying the damage, and it was surprisingly not total devastation. Not much left of the gear on deck; the mess gone, along with antennas, anchors, canvas top, half the varnish. The wheel bent, but still there. I lurched across the deck to steer again. Gooz, recovering, reassumed the role of fisher-captain.

"He's coming up! The loving charlie-tuna fish is coming! Gonna jump! He's gonna breach! Get Ready! *Backherdown!*"

I was on the point of yelling that I read somewhere giant tuna do not jump; but what did I know? I knew for certain, one thing, it was useless to argue with a man determined on self destruction.

His death wish was almost a visible aura now as a fiendish grin spread across his Stan Laurel mush and his electric hair was nearly buzzing with static fire. He was grinding on the big reel in fast forward, looking for all the world like a silent Ben Turpin flick, tongue out, head bobbing, but not keeping ahead of the fish.

The line was slack. I was hugging the wheel with one hand and a handrail with the other, braced with legs spraddled out against the rolling little boat.

But something ominous in the needles rushing up and down my skin. The giant wave bad enough, and we escaped. But now I had a John Wayne sense of doom, with a General Custer kind of oh-oh In my throat. Something grim and desperate about to happen to our ship. And its crew. The line was too slack. It was merely, I thought, the calm before the storm.

Gooz yelling again, singing, "From the Halls of Montezuma, to the shores of Tri..." He'd need a couple dozen marines to get us out of this.

Then his voice was drowned out by the rush of a rocket launching behind the boat – a huge, thick, black-bodied missile the width of a Greyhound bus and twice as long, with wrinkled grey-black skin and flippers sprung out on the sides like Sturm-flugles.

"Good gravy boat," I yelled. "Is that a whale on the port quarter?" Notice how fast I picked up the sailor's terms, as if it mattered if I'm right or not. I could just as quick said there is an old-faithful geyser blowing up behind us, for all the good it would do. But it was a not a geyser, except that on the top of its head where a cloud of spray was whooshing out, I could see it. But as it rose like a Macy's Day balloon and the body turned in a half twist nearing the top of its arc, I saw a baseball size red flaring eye focused squarely on the stern of Alvin Apfelbrot's sportfisher.

That eye was -- yeah, mad as hell.

That angry red eye looking down at us as the mammoth figure blotted out the sky above us; then I saw ... *the mullet*. It was hanging from the hook-gaff on the end of that big square nose. Harley Goosbladder had stuck his snag-hook into a genuine giant, a live blue whale. If I knew anything about the animal kingdom from my studies at Pottstown State University School of Veterinary Medicine, I knew one thing for sure:

It came to me in a flash as I watched the big black body curving up to the top of its leap in slow motion,

loom ing as a shadow cast by Judgement Day, floating down pulling the covers over our eyes, dropping like dusk,
square on top of Alvin Apfelbrodt's sportfisher.

The flash is, none of us mattered in this. Goosbladder's Krystal Creme Do-Nuts might never grace the table of America's breakfast anymore; I will not travel to attend Spring Break another time, or look up the tail end of an earthworm at Pottstown State University School of Veterinary Medicine.

The secret, the curse of Harley Goosbladder:
That giant genuine live blue whale was ...*absolutely mad as hell.*

To say everything turned black after the shades are pulled down is not to exaggerate. It was black for a long time, black and blue. All over big, good natured Harley Goosbladder and all over me, too, as we were lying in the Queen Elizabeth Hospital in Nassau in the Bahayma Islands, where they do indeed talk English not German.

Whatever that fish, that whale, did to Alvin Apfelbrot's boat is now just a blur, but I knew that because of Harley Goosbladder, Alvin was gonna be mad as hell, if nothing: else. But Gooz was not speaking about something elementary as that.

He was high as a kite, the notion occured to him as we were riding in the rescue basket of the Bahama Air-Sea Rescue Agency helichopper. He was talking about his fish. His world record catch on 180-lb. wire line. His unlimited world record that he could not even take back to Darmstadt, Wisconsin with him except in faint memory and an eye-witness description which I promised.

Because, after all, I survived this once-in-a-lifetime Spring Break adventure and found my life forever changed. That was my first boat trip; I knew I, too, was hooked on this stuff, even if I did not totally agree with Gooz's reasoning. But he was not put off with reason. His mind was made up; nothing ever would change it.

He slammed a ham-hand down on the hospital bed rail, and yelled, "I caught it! A fish inside the transom door is a landed fish!" He screamed it out so loud the room was soon filled with expectant nurses bearing loaded shots of tranquilizer.

"A World Record catch! It is the loving boat that is wrong. I ain't never gonna borrow nobody's boat no more. Especially from Alvin Apfelbrodt!"

I thought that last part was on the money. And I agreed out loud with Harley Goosbladder, because I decided to break his string. No matter what, he was not going to make me *mad as hell*.

Besides, I think not all fisherpersons in the record books have brought home all their fish. You just take their stories with a grain of salt. Right?

For instance, you take Heimingway. His Old Man did not get to eat his giant marlin, either. Or to even take it home.

And look at Jonah's great big fish. Think about it. Remember?

It ate *him*."

#

#

Seven

Pirates in Caribbean History

Capt. Abraham Blauvelt – as in 007's Dr. No -- Blofeld-- was a Privateer, Officer of the Swedish East India Company who preyed on Spanish ships. His headwaters and sphere soon became the route from New York to Jamaica, as well as plundering treasure ships off the coasts of Nicaragua and Honduras. Being unwelcome in Newport, Rhode Island, because of his reputation as a Pirate, he set out to find perhaps other places would accept him yet allow him to live the life he chose. He went south, and found what he was looking for in Central America. He somehow wound up living with the mystical Brazos Indians at Cape Gracias a Dios, in Nicaragua. There he took up with another Pirate, Captain Sir Christopher Myngs, and continued raiding the shipping out of Campeche, Mexico. His history disappears around 1663 and it is assumed he was lost at sea. His name, however, still graces the town of Bluefield, Nicaragua.

Up Voodoo Creek
Without a Paddle,
Nor Star to Steer by

Beware the scurvy Voodoo skullduggery

This guy was definitely not a surgeon, as Captain Kern had chronicled this escapade:

"Tondelayo wound her sensuous arms around my neck and rubbed the furnace of her breast against me. Her burning lips were at my ear, so close I could feel her tongue, though I had no idea of her words.

The beheading took only a single lightning swipe of the Pirate's cutlass. The *Lord Doctuh* hoisted the body, still convulsing, spilling scarlet. For me to see, specifically, the sacrifice showed his power over life, demonstrating death. No bother with 20 lashes to punish a hostage. His mouthful of yellow teeth grinned like a wolf. A hard lump suddenly constricted my stomach, like a gnarled fist.

A voice echoed deep inside me, *"To all passengers: This is not a drill!"*

Mystic, maybe, the *Doctuh*, like a big bluebottle fly. Red rimmed Hollywood shades, wraparounds, glowing lights of maybe two hundred votive-birthday candles dancing in their reflection.

Even so, dark as an oven in there, hot, smoky from a smudge fire, smoldering incense — or was that gorgonzola cheese. I could see long, skinny brown arms and legs poking out of a stained blue polyester robe. Underneath, he was, after all, a man.

I'm a reasonably stable person. Hardly ever do I doubt my own sanity, but this nightmare advancing on me displayed a definite plunge into the inferno. He could have been dangerous, or not, except in one hand he was clutching the writhing, headless chicken, and the other pointing straight at me with a grisly, curving Samovar blade.

I glanced at Felipe, the innocent who cringed on my right, in question. His hand touched my shoulder, he was trembling. His voice croaked, "This guy, she say he most potent Voodoo priest, maybe in whole world." Amen to that.

If not my whole life, surely my whole day began flashing before my eyes, and my most obscene question, after what rite was this priest about to commit with that sword, was, "How the Captain Blood did I get myself into this?" The story rambles on, dream into nightmare.

Answer: As strangely as the dawn breaks open the sky. With cellos.

The sun came wobbling up, bleeding like a golden pumpkin over the ragged, palm fringed bay. I ambled onto my back deck, fondling a mug of coffee in the cool morning mist. Green worms in my head from last night. Then I saw it.

Alright, World. Why are you picking me?

Nothing like a major loss to blast open a day in paradise, smack you in the gut, let you reel, helplessly in the wind. But, I already knew this:

Civilization ends at the waterline.

There was no doubt, that half-inch aircraft cable—enough steel to hoist a full grown humpback whale—was cut. Cloven. No nibbling. No hacksaw. Some Godzilla set of high-tech teeth swooshed by in the night, and without a second's pause, went *chomp*! Left me with ten feet of empty tether dangling off the stern of my trawler, *London Fog*.

Worse, my dinghy was attached. The cannibal on the cutting edge of those monster surgical shears had swum off with my whaler in its maw, plus a 15-horse Evinrude. About two thousand bucks worth, but more serious than just money. It left me crippled.

Any cruising boat owner will tell you, my dinghy is the last link to land, sometimes the most important. My dinghy is my pal, buddy, indispensable tool. It shepherds me out to the nearest lobster hole to bring home dinner. I anchor offshore any reef, rock, shoal, beach, or point of land; my dinghy waddles patiently astern, eager to do my wishes.

A dinghy hauls equipment, supplies, or crew to the local pub, town, or just walk on dry land. Without a dingy, a sailor is a cowboy sans stirrups, a farmer without a pick-up truck and no bus to town.

So, Fidel's bunch and Haitians are not our only *Caribbean Okies* seeking a better deal from whoever is up there, shuffling the cards.

Then in disguise as Puerto Ricans, they board the plane for legal entry into the U.S., Promised Land of Madonna, McDonalds, slick Japanese SUVs, MTV and

Saturday Night Live. They sign up for welfare and our generous SS program.

"You make their dreams come true," Felipe grins. He's such a dreamer.

Okay, I 'm a soft touch, a sucker for a hard luck story. But this saga was not signed and sealed just yet. It was too early to start swilling Pirate's grog, even to hammer down my sorrow, but I hung around the sun bathed streets, moping under achingly blue tropic skies, mulling over murder, weighing solutions.

Except for weather, there aren't too many solutions in that part of paradise. I saw Felipe approaching from down the street, with someone else, but I was preoccupied by the mix of my own loss and the local problems. Samana' was a failed tourist scheme, part of the D/R's huge imbalance of too many people, no jobs and not enough money.

Back in the middle 1960s, after U.S. Marines and the CIA slapped down a communist rebellion and restored democracy of sorts, President Joaquin Balaguer touched Uncle Sugar for a fistful of dollars, and, praying Samana' will be another *Cancun-style* tourist coup, with hoopla he built a fine, four-lane boulevard with overhanging street lights. He razed the city's poor shacks, made public housing.

He built new schools, even a tidy prison. And so President B commissioned ad campaigns to lure tourist money into the almost perfect bay where Columbus once landed 500 years back. Plenty of Pirates headquartered on that Spanish Main for two hundred years. They were the first tourists who "vacationed" in Samana. And that's more than old Admiral Cristobal did for the place way back when. He apparently left a crew there and went back to Spain by himself to plead with Ferdinand and Isabela for more money and ships. His main pursuit was gold, but apparently it wasn't the buried treasure in those fine hills. Money was always a problem there, as El Pres B realized when his modern plans grew bigger than his budget.

Alas, he had miscalculated: No money to build an airport. The closest was several bumpy hours away at Puerto Plata, another former Columbus hangout, which the Admiral named "*Silver Port*," with high hopes and little promise. Neither black-jacked the dealer.

I dragged myself down to the Policia Commandante's office to report. Capitano Oro smiled, ruefully. His smiling secretary filled out the papers. A ring of very bad people, he assured me, not typical Dominicans.

By now the noon sweat was trickling, so I sauntered into Wally's Bar to see if the sun might be over the yardarm, maybe in Munich. Felipe found me there, the thousand yard stare on my puss.

He slugged my arm. "C'mon, we gonna go get back your dinghy."

I didn't even look up. Rats. I figured some scum would seep out of the woodwork hallucinating with visions of reward plums, but Felipe... how could he?

I would be given first right of refusal for the contraband, sure, for a bargain price. I demanded a name, who scammed it? He wouldn't say. Then I saw he was not alone.

She slipped out from behind him, nubile, cinnamon skin, hair reddish brown, and brushed in a sleek cascade to one side. She smelled of coconut, and in my sailor's ever-hopeful observation, perhaps an aroma of Obsession cologne. Or was it Tabu? Took a moment for my gaze to quit her smoldering eyes, survey the balance, in a leopard print off shoulder blouse, short black skirt, floppy Peter Pan boots. "I, Tondelayo," she breathed.

The only English she spoke. Behind one ear she wore a giant red hibiscus flower.

Felipe said, "She take us to the guy who get back your dinghy," He insisted I go with him, on a little moped he rented. An unheard of extravagance. These people have zero money. He is dreaming, I grumble, of a payoff worth more than I am.

And the girl, this smoky princess whose eyes burned with passion even as she absently slid her fingers down my dripping beer bottle. How could she fit into this equation? Sure, I knew a few Dominican women in my brief pauses in their country. They are enchanting, especially in their youth, with lovely dispositions, and they like American men. This one seethed with everything a man could want, with only the barest hint of grim professionalism. It's no sin there. Daughters earn their keep.

I mounted up behind him on the tiny bike. Tondelayo sandwiched between us, a whiff of her tantalizing fragrance wafting over me. The mo-ped was hopelessly outgunned by our bulk, but popping and snarling, it ran through road and jungle.

Over the noise I yelled for Felipe to tell me where we were headed. He shook his head. Tondelayo would steer him.

We bumped and banged far out of the town into the wild, picturesque countryside, squirreling up steep mountain grades, down gravel roads, then dirt trails; zipped through grinding poor villages where squawking chickens darted across us; then teetered over a terrifying, vine-strung bridge, and finally a footpath through tangled lianas, as monstera leaves flapped and whacked at our shoulders and knees.

We were indeed in deep, fathomless jungle. Magnificent 100-year-old trees rose up seemingly higher than a ten-story office buiding, brushing the gourd-like cumulo-nimbus clouds, shutting out most of the glorious blue sky. Lush jungle crowded in on all sides, easily minimizing man's feeble attempts at so-called progress. Coconut, avacado, mango and other trees bore delightful snacks just for the plucking. No wonder the people stayed healthy.

Then at last, a clearing. Half a dozen thatched outhouses circled a sort of main hut. *Roll the cameras: Scene Three —Action! Hideout for pig thief Pirates, cocaine dealers, at the very least a marijuana packing plant.*

The big hut stood open, filled with women, giggling, stirring big pots. A cut from MacBeth? No, it's the cookhouse. In the outback, Dominicans use cookhouses separate from their sleeping quarters. Small, bronze, auburn haired, naked children all around, running, laughing, chasing small birds, some off-brand miniature chickens. Catch one, smack it on the head with a stick, snatch off its feathers, still kicking. The women waited, to cook these hapless little critters.

I assumed Tondelayo was a graduate of this academy. The cooking women surely knew her, and several bore a resemblance, though older and not as silken smooth. She chattered a word now and then and a woman would turn and smile in my direction.

I found a seat in what must be the town hall. The women stared after me. One of the bigger kids pranced nakedly in front of me, eyeing my clothes, my deck shoes, waving his stick. No doubt deciding if a wandering sailor was a suitable garnish. If I escaped with my life I could say it was a miracle, or at least a nice end to the day. Other people began to drift in. The jungle flock, gathering.

Felipe paced nervously; finally, fate beckoned. Tondelayo led me, soft handed, into a hut, a cramped, close, fetid, darkroom, size of a double outhouse. No windows. Total black inside but for a thousand tiny votive candles. Cigar smoke, foul, mixed with the odor of badly cured cheese, or.. feet? from somewhere in the haze. Felipe followed, wide eyed.

Lord Doctuh emerged. In a soiled royal blue robe covered with little silver stars, a red fez, his wraparound Hollywood eyeshades flickered with a thousand glittering flames. The robe sported intricate embroidery, gold thread. His gaping grimace showed a golden glyph set in one of his yellow incisors. Not smiling, waved his arms, swimming to some song of the islands, perhaps some overture; hypnotic rhythm. Obviously we were onto the head roller in this crap shoot.

Felipe stared in total awe. I thought at any moment he might fall on his knees to worship. *His Holiness* ignored him. The quarry was me.

I thought of friends who begged to come on this trip, to taste the thrill of outre places, other peoples. Wherever I am, the bizarre will find me.

The priest rattled off two or three paragraphs of machinegun *espanol* at me. Unintelligible. He produced the live chicken from under his robe, and with a flourish, unsheathed the death-dealing cutlass.

I stared back, dumbly. What the hell does this plot have to with a dinghy theft ring? He had to be the head of it, an Al Capone clone, Godfather, a demonic success motivator.

Stealing dinghies, a way of life. Setting up perilous black moon crossings in stormy seas for people who will risk even death for a better chance at life. I bless the advantage of being born in the right place. I despise what the rest of the world must contend with. But look, do not burden me with ceremony. The next step would decide the extent of extortion; the price of the pudding. Felipe rattled back at him.

"Hey," I growled, "if I have to buy it back, let's get it on."

With a lightning strike, the shaman shrieked a curse, and severed the hapless chicken's head. He sashayed towards me, blood spurting, blade pointed at my throat.

Tondelayo's arm slid around my neck and her soft lips caressed my ear. Her voice was quick and very insistent, but her words went totally over my ken. Her hot breast singed my chest and I suddenly realized my hand was locked onto her slender waist.

Felipe snapped me out of it. He was a believer. "She say," he rasped, "this most powerful voodoo priest in all Santo Domingo. His curse so vile, so evil, horrible, on him who steal your dinghy, within one week his spell force them to bring it back."

"Yeah?" I say, dawn breaking, "How much for the curse?"

"Twenty dollars U.S. two hundred fifty pesos."

"A week is too long," I countered. "I want to leave for Puerto Rico tomorrow. How much for say, an Overnight U.P., or Fed-X, curse delivery?"

Felipe rolled his eyes. "Is not simple. With Voodoo, you under *Lord Doctuh's* will. He say, you go back to boat, you dip glass of water where dinghy now absent. You bring. He mix holy water. Then make evil spell."

Turned out the fastest curse guarantee would be three days, and that would run a mere 700 pesos. "Okay. Deal," I snapped. I've never learned how to negotiate, especially in another country .

Inevitably, I am just another of those little birds, naked, waiting to be plucked, alive.

Tondelayo's fingers caressed me, lips nibbling at my ear. Felipe translated: "She say, money nothing to you, wealthy man. You pay, you win important thing." Hormones into the mix.

Finally, it was time to choose. Okay, but no money up front, I ventured. This miracle can only be wrought C.O.D. Felipe frowned. High Priest scowled.

He slammed the chicken into the dirt. Tondelayo slid off my lap and darted for the door, behind the High Priest. He swung his saber after her, spitting, "Puta!"

"Hey pal," I said, backing out, "money cannot buy believers."

We mounted up and mo-peded out of *His Holiness'* pasture, through a swelling crowd of parishioners. They were queuing up, taking numbers for an audience; a curse, a cure, a favor from *Lord Doctuh*. Later, Wally, who runs the American Bar in town, begged me for his name, for casting spells – or a few incurable diseases — on his debtors.

I had dug in my heels, I would not pay, directly against Felipe's warning. Yet the Voodoo spell, or something, wreaked its results in record time. When I went for clearance papers to Puerto Rico, the Commandante's boys converged. They had recovered my dinghy. There, on the front lawn it sat, what was left of it. Hallelujah, almost.

Soldiers in a truck trundled in with the culprit. A fisherman who "found it," expected a reward, was in deep dungeon. Crowed Capitano Oro, "Here is Jefe (chief) of the theft ring!"

My little boat, alas, was unrecognizable. They had stripped off all her hardware, sawed the motor off her transom, discarded the mangled hulk to drift to the beach. Not even a paddle. Total wretchedness. Too ugly to hate I rigged a tow line, said my goodbyes, tipped Felipe ten bucks, and at dawn dropped the lines to ship out. My last sight of Samana was Tondelayo, sprinting down the pier, travel bag in hand, entreating me for a ride to the good life. But there is no escape from reality, I called to my promised one.

I sicced *London Fog* out of the paradise bay and by dusk made a freebooter's crossing of the Mona Passage between Hispaniola and Puerto Rico. A narrow strait rushing between islands, like the Gulfstream, feared as one of the world's most dangerous transits.

After a lumpy night in the Mona (that's 'monkey' in Spanish), I looked at my wake. The towing harness splashed across the morning glow of sunrise. And at its end, nothing.

My dinghy had given up its ghost in some 2,000 feet of blue Caribbean. So, Felipe, you dirt bag, you were right? It could turn on me, he warned:

"You no pay, the Executioner's spell,
It become a curse."

But all was not lost. In the morning paper at Boqueron, P/R, salvation. A small ad promised a "dinghy and motor, complete, $1,500." My kind of deal. In a borrowed pickup truck I drove to the north coast, Loquillo, for my new dime-store dinghy. Very light weight, but a bargain's a bargain. Back at Boqueron, I launched it, stepped in. Floor boards trampolined under my feet. I felt the Voodoo bete noire sniff, darkly, in the shadows.

By ten minutes into its maiden voyage, disaster loomed. The transom teetered, crazily, the seats came unglued, hull flexed like paper towels. I had bought a biodegradable boat!

I hauled it in, slathered it heavily stem to stern with epoxy glue. Next day, doggedly, nosed *London Fog* around the bend of P/R, bound for picturesque Puerto Patillas, a funky in-grown fishing village, dinghy in tow with a hognose stainless steel ring in her prow.

As a precaution, I removed the outboard engine. A stroke of prophecy. An evil wind sprang up immediately, with churning waves. Hungry seas began to gnaw at my little beastie. Chunks of it were slipping away beneath the brilliant blue. The flotation box broke loose. One by one, the seats drifted off and were quickly devoured. The deck began to undulate in the ocean's ravenous mouth. Another five miles, I turned to check, and I was struck by an awful truth:

It is over, indeed, when the flat dinghy sinks.

My new pal was nowhere in sight. Fluttering in my long, frothy wake-trail was only the tow-ring, burbling freely in the salt spray. The curse.

But Felipe, that dog, had told me Voodoo works only if you accept it. I plumbed my psyche, in depth, and dredged up no pangs of conversion.

I am not a believer! I reject You, Voo! Doo! Shoo! Yet now, with every salty mile the villainous witchcraft hex lingered at the back pocket of my Levi's cut-offs.

For eternity in these islands, I feared, I was doomed to guard my soul (and my next dinghy) against this evil shadow, forever lurking in my sea-going path, its haunting legend as my epitaph:

Heed Capt. Kern's advice: Pay the Witch Doctor his due, or you, too, may be zeroed in on:
As part of the food chain.

#

Capt. Chuck Gnaegy

Eight

Pirates in Caribbean History

Mary Read, always tied with Anne Bonny as the most storied, if not the only female pirates, was a formidable buccaneer herself. Raised as a boy by her mother, she ran away to sea on a Man-o-War. A true adventurer, she then jumped ship and fought in Flanders with a Horse Regiment, where she met and later married a fellow soldier. He died, but her adventurous spirit urged her on. She went to sea again, hooking up with Pirate Calico Jack Rackham. There she also tookup with Anne Bonny. Then she found a man she wanted; but he had been challenged to a duel by another pirate. She interposed and took on the bigger pirate. More agile and quicker, she tripped him, and when he fell, ripped open her blouse to expose her breasts. That cunning ruse stunned him for a second; so Mary's cutlass whistled, slashing his throat. Later, with Bonny, thrown in jail by the Governor for Piracy, she died of a fever in 1724.

The Jaguar Conspiracy

A *Modern Buccaneer's Plot for Millions in Gold*

It promised to be the most bizarre voyage I'd ever embark upon.

Prince Igor had me standing there like a dunce. Outside a summer storm was getting ready to dump its backwash on the funky island of Key Largo. The Prince had backed himself behind a fountain at the Italian Fisherman restaurant and was talking from a vantage point that kept his back to the wall, out of sight.

I was standing in front of the fountain, so it looked to any passerby that I was talking to a naked statue, a marble kid who was pee-ing into the fishpond, like at that French shrine.

Lightning flashed, thunder rumbled. Prince Igor's blue gum-ball eye swept toward me like a frozen cocktail onion with a black center. Dead serious, he sounded as though he was correcting the kid in potty training:

"Prince Igor hass got to deliver a spezial shipment into the jungle. Guatemala. Rio Dulce. By boat. How qvick you are ready to go?"

Right to the point, the Prince. I liked the way he talks in second person. I wonder if he recognizes it's him. But he was not telling me all of it.

"Uhm," I said, "What kind of stuff would you say is in this shipment?"

"Prince Igor would say this... gung...be heavy," he stated imperially, slowly nodding from his towering stature. "Ver heavy, and I sink zee airline does not want to strap it under his wing and tie a saddle onto. Szo! How soon you go?"

"Not fooling with preliminaries, huh Prince? But he, should tell me the contents."

A burst of wind surged through, flapping his salt and pepper hair. His wooly bear eyebrows shot up. "Why should he?"

"Plenty of reasons for not going in there. For example, gorillas in the hills, and federales in the valleys. Pirates on the Spanish Main. Maybe you're sending in camo-painted machine guns, some nuke surprises for the government. I hear they are chasing around the country-side like a Central American banana rebellion. And some CIA types on either side. Or both sides, as the case may be. And Prince, being the modern Buccaneer..."

"Capitano" he murmured softly, addressing a two year-old. "Prince Igor hire you drive ship, not analyze political spectrum. Do not forget to whom you speak. Prince Igor owns enough scenarios in your past to make a fat page of testimony, especially ATF, Alcohol Tobacco & Firearms people, U.S. Customs, not to mention Coast Guard..."

The first patter of rain plopped on Florida Bay, behind us. "So," I said, "you'll blackmail me into some African Queen river run to Guatemala? What's the cargo?"

His eyes blinked, slowly, owl wise, and I feared he

was going to reach and scratch my ears. "Extraordinar-ily spezial shipment. Not to be discovered by local authorities, national agencies, Interpol. No one."

He withdrew a gold matchbook from his silk jacket, and with great ceremony removed a gold-headed match. He struck it. We were both transfixed as gold flame leapt.

"You see, the man who holds the cards gets to say the name of the game."

"Uh, wait a min…" I was beginning to close in. He was into heavy metal. "You telling me there is some-body in this thing, that if we do not succeed…"

The Prince snuffed out the match. "Eggs-act-ly." The smoke whisped up, shakily, then whiffed away as a frigid wind puffed through.

An ice cold frog slithered up my backbone. "Hey, Prince, I think if you want me to take this on, I ought to know *what*. Huh?"

His marble eyes went flat. His voice was ice water "No."

"Maybe it's ransom money? Bribe? Terrorism? I won't do it."

He leaned forward, addressing me, Viceroy to foot-man. "I vant you take two million dollars gold into Guatemala jungle."

The value sprang to my brain. I couldn't cope with the details. "But... why gold?" I stammered "The bank is willing, for a small fee, to transfer as much money to your account as you have in it. I've done this plenty of times when I was stuck in a foreign - friendly or no. A simple international wire..."

"Capitano, you do not see the lightning. The guy holding the ace, a top executive from General Bananas.

He decide he does not listen to reason. No foreign currency of any kind. No local currency under any circumstances. No government, no Interpol, no noone."

Lightning cracked with a zzzt and simultaneous boom. I jumped straight up. A waiter stumbling toward me hefted a huge tray of wine glasses and a lighted candle. I saw it in slo-mo. Smoking ominously, the tray tilted toward the Prince, who leapt sideways, as the waiter fell forward, tray swooped at statue. There was a white light explosion as the waiter's shoulder nudged me forward and the naked marble kid toppled into the drink.

When the smoke cleared, Prince Igor was gone. The statue had me pinned in the pool, and in the sea of faces staring down at me I didn't see one friend, only the irate owner pointing at the statue. Waiter explained the fault was not his. He was short and squat and I had never seen him prior. Trouble has its way to find me.

Before I could react, a commotion behind the group was stirred up and I heard the little-girl voice yap, people get out of the way. Boopsie. The nick of time. She rushed to me.

"I saw the whole thing!" she cried. "A strange foreign type of man pushed this waiter into my darling here, and I think we ought to sue for damages from the management!"

Someone in the crowd said, "Yeah, I saw it too. This weirdo, talking to the statue!"

The manager saw a further genuine storm brewing that could cost big bucks.

"Awright, Captain Crutch," he knew me, "get the yuck out of here before I do call the sheriff." He hauled the waiter out of the pond. "Get that stuff cleaned up."

Later, Boopsie and I were relaxed after a shower and the preliminaries. "What?"

"I guess I should not tell you."

"Then I'm going home, Now."

"Aw, Boops…"

"Tell me."

"I've got to take two million dollars in gold into the Guatemalan jungle."

She screeched. "Two million big ones? That is too heavy to fit into a briefcase. It must be about ten thousand pounds worth."

"Not even close. Only 12 troy ounces to a pound of gold. Maybe six hundred. And gold is now $30 and might go to $300 an Oh-zee? You do the math. Maybe it flexes enroute.

"Okay, then," she breathed, grinned, whistled, her nimble tongue poking in and out of her sweet cupids-bow mouth. "Is this some kind of spook stuff? When do we leave?"

"Ugh, maybe," I said. "I don't know yet.It's a thing I never think of. To me , gold comes in chains. Teeth. Spoons. Not bulk. Ransom." What kind of kook thing could this be? It could be on one side, either side, or both sides as the case may be.

It was a long, sweaty September. 1 was tied up at the dock in Key Largo. My 51-foot ketch *Pleasure Me* was totally attached to land, with a full set of long snaky umbilicals trailing off her stern to bring aboard civilian style, life giving electric lights, air conditioning, and H2o, like a well bred condominium.

I had not yet swallowed the anchor or grown to the bottom, but there was a suspicious green pallor hanging off my keel. I was resting up for whatever came next, and interviewing prospective first mates. In case I might decide to charter.

In this context I was at Coconut's Bar just down the pier, lading on a fresh supply of rum-runners, while current Lady First Mate Candidate – who thinks Betty Boop is too cool— awaited on the afterdeck for her innerview. She was wearing this teensy peach patch bikini. Adding to her already overall peachiness, she was squealing happily to any and all who passed by, in her teensy little Betty Boop voice.

The sun dropped behind the yardarm into the trumpet vines, and I was slogging back to the yachet with a fresh supply of happy juice frozen pink. A dozen steps away I realized B Boop was going to get her first test on electronic gear. The radio/com phone contraption beeped, red-lit, ready to fire off, and her eyes flashed, saucer size.

"Is that a phone? How do you work that thing?" she squealed, obviously not a child of the machine age. "A cell phone? Which button?"

"Punch 'Intercept,'" I said, realizing that one does not hire a First Mate on mechanical skill alone. "Uh, never mind. I'll get it. But take a couple of these strawberry icicles off my hands, which are about to weld me into frozen glassware."

The machine gulped, snuffled, took a deep breath, and clucked its tongue. F/M candidate was plainly not terrified. "Is that phone thing about to toss its cookies?"

No F/M is ever perfect, I decided, and that gives the masculine psyche a pleasant jolt of superiority. But if she can't dig ATT, it will be monumentally tough to dredge her through GPS, RDF, SAT/NAV, SSB, 13WPM/

CW; + a stack of foreign currencies we don't know.

"Maybe it just needs a shot of dramamine. You can Ignore it." I juggled the tray of pink passionsickles on the taffrail, trying to climb onto the stern. The tide was in, and the first step was a high pitch. Before I could get it, the machine spake, slowly, cultured, masculine: "Dahzvidania, Vanya. A riddle: If a ship of the desert navigates the eye of a needle, can a yacht captain float a package of life savers into the Temple of the Jaguar? Four one, eight two, eight three, dash, one four, one five, eight six, three seven, minus one."

Machine stopped. Gulped. Clicked. Dial tone.

"What the beep was that all about?" Boopsie chirped. "Are you some kind of spook? Is that Russian code for the end of the world?"

"I, as you can see, am only a simple boat captain," I assured her.

"Then who is that nutcake there?" She plunged a straw into the nearest rum runner and evacuated it. She giggled, a wiggling delight. "Nutball telephone calls? What a boat. Was he on whoopy snort?"

"Not likely, " I countered, bobbling the tray. "Play it back while I stash the rest of these frozen pink perils in the freezer."

I have stock for a whole rosy evening sunset panorama. Why trot back and forth for refills — in case F/M/C Boopsie, if she gets over her machine fetish, proves interesting.

"One more time, if you please. Play it again, Pam, and take down the numbers."

"Which button? Which button?" she demanded, stabbing at random. The machine clicked frantically.

I could see Boop will have to be very interesting to overcome her total lack of mechanical aptitude. "Uh, Press Replay." She poked at it, sloshing blobs of strawberry R&R over all. It blinked off, panting.

"Oh! I've busted it. You'll never trust me again with your personal equipment."

I was not touching that statement with a ten foot spinnaker pole. I reached around her, got the machine moving again, and instructed her to try one more time.

She played it again, Sam, little lines formed on her forehead. "What it is, some bozo-nut getting Jolly rolls on a tape recorder? Is he some kind of Prussian?"

I chuckled. While it could be some nuthatch, it could just as easily be some borderline case who talks in riddles, of which I know a goodly number. I gulped some strawberry pink and eyed her. "What do you think?"

"Booby hatch time," she mumbled; and I thought B/B more fetching when she didn't speak than when she squealed. She would never understand. But I did. As I suspected all the time, this was to be a case of riddle-me-rich.

"Well," goes B/B, "what does it all mean?"

"Prince Igor."

"Huh? What is that? Why does he talk like that?"

"A friend. With a charter. Wants me to call him back. Unlisted number. You take it down?"

"Huh? What I wrote down? 418283-14158673? That's a phone Number?"

"Minus one. Equals 377-0072. See? He has a penchant for double-O numbers. His background. The 'minus one' is the code. See...?"

"Well," she wiggled saucily, in her perpetual pout,

Actually, it was a typical message from Prince Igor. I considered not telling Boopsie the whole truth, but I could see there would be repercussions. And it could cost me a whole evening of long lower lip, despite frozen pink panthers. So, either spill the beans or spend the night waiting for BB to come out of the closet. So I'd go for the gold.

"Prince Igor is Russian. He is always careful to announce he is a White Russian, though I cannot think how many other colors they might have there. Something about his heritage, he says, which I gather makes him a bit closer to God than all of us.

"His father was fifth in line for the Russian Czarist throne. Prince speaks five or six languages including Russian and Mandarin Chinese, and English better than most people I know. He spent assorted years of his life in clandestine operations for Uncle Sugar. Cloak and dagger. James Bond could carry his suitcase. Everything he does is in riddles. But that is all over now, even with the Cold War gone forever. Now he's a "Security Consultant."

"So, that makes him something?" Boopsie demanded. "So, what's his real name, anyway?"

I spell it slowly so even B/B gets it. "His real name is like the menu on a French restaurant where they slip you London broil in a new sauce: *Prince Igor Andreivitch Konstantine Alexiev Borzoi.*

"However, it is Americanized by his uncle— not Sam, but Uncle Crown Prince of all ByeloRussia, to Prince Igor Constantine. As a friend, he lets me call him by his first name."

"So which one is that?"

"Prince. Hahaha!"

It was beginning to sink in. "You mean," she squealed, "he really is a Russian Prince?" Now she has eyes for him already. The fickality of the femme fattail.

"Hmm. Yeah, except we do not have royal blood in the US of A, and don't recognize kings and stuff either."

"Mmm-hmm." She was grinding away on it. Thoughtful. Silent. Wheels were moving the Wabash Cannonball in her head. I can tell when a woman smells royal blood, or money, even if the rest of us are too dim-witted to recognize potential. She can already feel the tiara. "Geez, a Prince. Why can't a prince just say what he wants?"

I smile a wry return. "Prince Igor does not ever, just say what he wants. I think that too is a part of his heritage. I have to wring it out of him."

So, a simple leap from an interview to a phone call to a closeted conversation with the Prince, who is nursing his negative reaction to my demand to know all.

Next: We're hunkered down again, beside a potted palm at Italian Fisherman, some distance away from the naked kid statue. He whispers:

"Remove your boat from Key Largo, after midnight, and sail up to Biscayne Bay … here." He pointed a mani-cured digit to a spot on the chart, marked with a circled dot.

"You will prepare your ship for a journey. One thousand miles. Provisions. Navigation systems. Crew. In two days, dark of the moon, you will hear from me.

"Do not notify anyone here of your departure. Meet here, at Black Caesar's Creek."

I know the spot. Where Black Caesar – the once

notorious outlaw – had bottomed out his boat on the coral nobs and splashed away on foot, hiding behind his beard. Not a very bright disguise, if you ask me. Of course he didn't. Now I am going to use the same canal to start out; perfect for an under the counter escapade with a professional spook.

I nodded. "You are gonna like my crew."

He slipped me a wad of fifty dollar bills.

Caesar's Creek is a winding, deep inlet through a shallow flat, which leads finally to a rock wall dock space south of Miami. It was a long time favorite smuggler's hideout and may still be. It is not often patrolled by regular rounds of badge keepers, and is still a way to get into shore with a deep keel without attracting too much attention.

We arrived at dark of the moon. Gave a blinking light signal to await Prince's arrival. He didn't want me to dock at the high rock wall. I dropped a small kedge anchor. Lights out. Soon, we heard muffled voices; a very large, fat, inflatable boat inching toward us. "Pssst," Prince's disguised voice. "You haf to make a bosun chair so I can pass you these bricks." Under a large tarp.

Filled to the gunnels with, it looked like, building bricks. So loaded when he drew alongside I was sure he would capsize. Lucky there was no wind, or wakes from passing cowboys. Wood insert floor bowed up ridiculously at each end. I saw he was not alone.

Is this crazy? It was the gold, painted black, and stacked up. Each brick weighs about 75 lb. I am no mathematical whiz, but if my addition was anywhere close, $2 mil in gold would weigh something over 500 lbs., if not 5,000.

Plus 2 big guys in that boat, there was at least 1,000 pounds of pure gold and blubber in that fat, plastic blow-up kiddie pool.

"Hey, Prince," I whispered. "You want to make it look casual, don't you. Did you consider what happens if that load punches, sinks to the bottom?

"It would be easy to find."

"Yeah, unless you're in mud. Let's see, an ingot… brick , weighs about 75 pounds. Drops in mud four feet deep. Riddle, How do you slurp it out of there?"

"Nefer mind. Zey are in half- bricks. Chust rig your halyard and get it aboard." Boopsie was all pop eyes with adventure. "Is he really a Prince?" she squeeled.

In minutes, we had solved part of the problem. Half -bricks weigh less than 40 lbs. each. Not quite too hard to handle. Still a lump sum. Enough to decorate our own boatfull of Yellow Brick Road.

They are carefully trundled up and stowed aboard, in the bilge.I wondered why Prince didn't mold them like ballast. Loaves of bread. Scrap iron. If a Customs guy...

 Prince was very tense. He met Boopsie, who curtsied embarrassingly and asked for his autograph. He just stared at her, then rolled his blank martini olive eyes at me.

He brought aboard a new man, Gandolfo Gutierez. "Call me GeeGee." A short, compact, muscular Guatemalan with long black hair and a constant grin. Like a campesino gorging on pork roast, hiding a guilty secret, or just passing a lot of gas. Said nothing.

How did I get this motley crew? Was I the only

sane person here, or the craziest?

No matter. Time to get underway. I weighed the small kedge and fired up the diesel. We wound through Caesar's Creek and in no time were at sea, still inside the Gulfstream, heading S, then SW, for Cayo Oueste. Our course would pass Key West by next afternoon, cross the Gulfstream and sail westward along the north coast of Cuba. Then hug the Yucatan coast south to Livingston, Guatemala, and Rio Dulce, where we'd enter Lago de Izabal, our rendezvous point.

And so, off on our voyage of … riskcovery.

Prince stayed holed up in his stateroom, with a wracking cold, bronchitis, gurgling, hacking away night and day. He couldn't even speak to me about this operation, or outline his plan for what happens when we reach the fabled Rio Dulce, inMexico.

GeeGee took his post on deck at the bowsprit as if awaiting borders. Grinning so much there must be bugs in his teeth. If he was armed … well concealed, even from us. I suspected he was a Guatemalan government watchdog; knew more about the story of this voyage to the yellow brick road than I. He handled the wheel when I took naps.

Boopsie did the cooking and breathlessly tried to interest Prince in her food, which he hardly touched. I heard her chirping like his mother, "Eat, just try this, you'll like it. It's good for you!" That he was really sick was the fact he took no interest in her peach blonde bikini. She was now wearing cut-offs to see if he'd comment.

Autopilot on *Pleasure Me* took care of the steering and navigation. I checked our progress, gauges, the fuel consumption, radio net weather constantly. Light going, in beautiful sunshine days and moonglow nights. Lucked out on weather, hooray. We were motrosailing along, slopping at a crisp seven knots in our undercover mode, looking for all like a pleasure boat with a runaway-from-care Captain and crew, living the good cruising life. No one would suspect what rested in our hold.

Passed Key West and arrived off Cuba to make a right turn down the coast. We stayed 15 miles out, three miles past the International line which Cuba claims as her waters.

Evening, just past dusk, our shadow appeared, A lone white vessel, gunboat flying the flag of Cuba drew into range, a thousand yards back, in our wake. Gunship. Machine gun mounted on the foredeck. He followed all night, and a full day, tracing our exact course; hound dog on the scent of a Whopper. Could he know? Would he stop us? I kept track on radar, and I knew he did the same. A tense, worrisome time. For once I had a Spanish linguist speaker on board, even if alien to them. If they stopped us, which they had no legal right to do, and attempted to board, I'd call the U.S. Coast Guard. Aerial support, you bet.

But if there was a confrontation, Coast Guardies would also board my boat. A no-no. I've been boarded too many times in past voyages. I have come to appreciate and trust our young men who come to this job from Nebraska or Oklahoma, or Utah, knowing nothing about the sea or boats. They come clomping on board with their boots, half a dozen of them with U.S. of A. automatic weapons leveled at us, most likely they are scared to death, too. Still, they line everybody up against the wall and we crew or charters stand there until they're done.

Their usual modus-operandi, go through the vessel, dump out drawers, lockers, dig into the bilge, cabinets, hatches, tool boxes, lazarette, drag out everything they find and dump it on the deck, until they find no drugs. Then they leave. No apologies.

"You're free to go," they say, not mentioning I am also free to spend hours shoveling up this stuff, put back together what the Coast Guard puts asunder. Then sail on, to wait for the next "inspection," They do not even talk to each other on the radio.

We cruisers joke about how they would react if we, in dead of night, forced our way into their home – my vessel is my home – and performed the same type of search, without probable cause? I respect it is their duty; I don't protest.

One inspection I asked the young lieutenant in charge, "Of a hundred stops like this, how many result in a charge, or an arrest for transporting drugs… what's your percentage?. Fifty percent?" "No." "Ten?" "No." "Five?" "No." "One percent?" "Less than that."

No wonder they don't try to put it back together. Our guardians of the seas spend endless hours tearing apart civilians' boats, without even a reason for suspicion, except that we were there. And a laughable record of bringing down the drug trade. Semper Fi, guys. Maybe some dark night I'll need your help. Stay tuned.

The Cuban gunboat, meanwhile, trailed off at the junction of the Yucatan Channel, having given us our freedom, or their aegis.

We change course, a couple of points off due south.

We slipped past the charming, tiny Isla Mujeres, where the townsfolk are lining up at the taco factory for breakfast bread, then Cozumel, the dive capital, off starboard, and in one more day we sight the entry to Barrios, then Livingston, at Baya de Arnatique.

This bar can be very shallow at low water. We were at high tide. Inside, Lago Izabal okay. A Guatemalan Customs launch escorted us. Tied up, I gathered ship's papers and passports. I whispered to Boopsie, headed to the office.

They were very cordial, checked out documents and passports. I saw they were very interested in at least one of them. Could it be they recognize GeeGee? Or Prince Igor? Could they know the plot? If so, I feared a battalion of AK47 cops would descend, tie us up hand and foot, not reading us our rights as they do on NYPD Blue. I did not savor the prospect of a Latin American jail, from what I hear. Or could it be exactly what I was thinking, as they gaze, slobbering at Boopsie's photo? They stamped and returned the goods. Then demanded, very politely, that I conduct them to the boat, for an "inspection." Could I say no? My knees were kadidalling.

GeeGee, at his post on the bow, rattled espanol I couldn't make out, but didn't move from his perch. They ignored him. Prince Igor, coughing, hacking, trying to dredge up a bucket of phlegm that he could spew over the side, they avoid.

I showed them to the deckhouse. They entered warily, expectant; Boopsie understood my message. Tripped lightly from the galley. Peach flavored bikini. Blonde hair piled high on top her head. Full makeup.

Right off the poster in a mechanic's garage. She carried a tray of shrimp and lobster, ice cold Corona beers. Stunning vison for any man.

She giggled, "Welcome, Senior Customs gentlemen. I hope you will join us in a few tasty little snackeritos." She put the tray down on the big table and curtsied. Picked up a bottle of beer and handed it to the guy in charge.

"Bone appeteet," she chirped. "My Spanish is not so hot. In fact, it is non-existent." She gave it the toy doggie wiggle.

"That is quite alright," Mr. Customs #1 answered, mouth gaping open at her cantaloupes. "We are happy to converse with you in English." He gazed down at her peaches, and she leaned forward, pretending to arrange the snacks with her pretty manicured fingers, so he got a better eyeful.

His dark eyes bugged out. Whatever you say about Boops, she has the goodies to tantalize a man, and she executed this little tease play extremely well, like a top quarterback psyches out the 300-lb. Defensive End. Peach colored all over, in her teeny flesh-pink bikini, So precious you wanted to pick her up and squeeze them right then and there.

She turned to the Customs #2. "I hope you'll join in a refreshment, Senior." Flashed him the big grin, handed him a moist beer bottle. Rolled her eyes. I thought he'd drop to his knees any second.

"You like to see the rest of our nice yacht?" she offers. "I am happy to show you around." She flounced off to the passageway and clicked down the long hall, beckoning them. "This is one of our staterooms, and the hea – baaathroom, with a shower."

She had sprayed her cologne in the staterooms and head. The Customs guys took a whiff that made their heads spin. "We have two of these, and three staterooms, she chirped. Can I get you another beer…a serve-vaissa?" She giggled. "I know one word in Spanish! But that is the only one."

She beamed, posing at the stateroom door where the full cologne aroma drifted out.

"Yes, it is very attractive, very attractive," said Customs #1, eyelids fluttering. Sweat beaded on his upper lip. He wanted to spoil her rotten. He stuttered, "We are happy to inspect your yacht. Thank you very much."

He moved to the deckhouse. He was weak at the joints. "I think we shall be leaving now. We wish you a happy voyage and nice visit to our beloved Guatemala."

Boopsie handed them, as they debarked, a fresh bottle of Tequila Prima, the rarest variety, curtsied again.

They stumbled off to their own private museum of disappointment, never knowing what a giant coup they missed. All they would dream of in those wee morning hours with a man's virility at its greatest; Peachy you know who. She made their day, or month.

My indiscreet secret cargo had slippered its way through another road-net like a river eel. And we were cleared into the foreign country to deliver an obscene two million dollar massage to … whom?

I did not even know.

That was more and more complicated, the deeper we got. Prince emerged from his stateroom at last. He looked like a moth out of its cocoon, alive but very weak and needing a double shot of cafe latte, with a booster of chocolate liqueur. He blew his nose, loudly.

"Vee are coming to Za Good Part," he whispered, nasally.

"Well, suppose you let us in on some of it, before Vee Get Zere," I said. "I'm beginning to be annoyed by this dark secrecy, it involves all of us."

"In time," he rasped.

"Hey, Prince," I snapped, "we are all in this together. Now either you tell me what goes down, or I ..."

He grabbed my arm. "You are be-ink impatient, Capitano. In time."

By nightfall we had traversed the wide bay and into the Rio Dulce, the 'sweet river.' Winding sinuously past jungled islands peppered with white and black anhingas, they were draped from the trees, drying their spread-out wings like a herd of hemophiliac vampire bats. Howler monkeys hooted at us, following tree to tree. What? Throwing balls of monkey caca at us. Welcome to life in the primitive, guys. Top pecking order rules.

Evening descended mysteriously. The moon rose, a yellow-ochre full blown giant lemon, blossom of the jungle river, over the up-raised adoring arms of coconut palms. In that filtered glow, we saw the structure, rising out of the jungle, perhaps ten stories high, built in block sections, giant square-hewn stones piled high into the sky, reaching to a tapered peak. Moved to the foredeck , deepening moonlight to view the tropical phenom.

"Oooo-oo-hhh," Boopsie murmured. "If that was not so eerie, I'd think it is mysteriously bee-yoo-tee-ful.

Is this where we are going? What is this thing?"

"I do not know," I confessed. "A Mayan monument from the beginning of time. Created even before Egypt knew where the rocks were."

"It isss," the gurgly voice of Prince came from behind us, "Za Temple of za Jaguar."

"Wheee!" Boops twittered, "The Prince is alive! Are we there yet, Princie Baby?"

"Vee are Zere. Yess."

The drill was simple enough. Rendezvous with the contact. Transfer the gold. Slip down Rio Dulce and back to the good old Yew Ess of A. We are then out of it. Home free.

But… it is not over until the fat red macaw squawks.

We slid forward in the river cautiously, until we rounded a wide bend. Depthfinder told me we were in the channel, but there is skinny water on the side where the temple is. No way in. Our cargo has to go ashore in the dinghy.

I informed Prince. Didn't like it. I saw, even in this light, the blood rising to his big cheeks. His ears on fire. He wanted me to risk my boat and take it to the small dock there.

I refused. "There is no water. We get stuck in there, no way out, either."

"But, you must take it in zere, to za dock."

"No."

"I vant you to take it in!"

"That was not part of the deal, Prince, and you know it. I cannot take my boat into that shallow water. I cannot leave it while I row your stuff in. I won't do it."

He stamped his feet. "I do not vant to go!"

I ignored him. Instead, I went below, opened the wide floorboards, and rigged the halyard to haul out the gold bricks through the forward hatch. GeeGee was there, grinning, on deck to receive it. The transfer took some time. We were hot and sweaty. Boopsie was pouring icewater for us, and pulling perfumed tissues from a little fanny pack, wiping our faces. That felt nice. Eyes as big as frisbees at all that plunder, again.

Prince paced the deck, rummaging his princely mind to find a solution. There was one, or None.

Finally we had it loaded into the fragile dinghy. Floorboards bowed up again like a mahogany potato chip. I pulled the dinghy around to the stern.

"Okay, Prince, it's time for you to wade in with your cargo."

He hauled out a small pistol. "I vant you to take ziss cargo in."

"No."

He brandished the gun. "I do not say please."

"Prince, now come on. You don't want to do this. A gun is dangerous stuff."

He held it, pointing upward, elbow bent, like I saw on old Police Story videos with Angie Dickinson.

"I know," he growled.

Suddenly I slapped my wrist up, across his forearm, knocking the gun upward. It fired! A shot deafening us at that close range. I wrapped my hands around his arm and twisted the gun loose. It clattered to the deck where, quicker than you can follow, Boopsie swept in and swooped it up.

She did not scream, but leveled the piece at GeeGee,

who halted in mid leap at me. "Stop right there, Mr. G.G.! And you too, Mr. Prince." She did not chirp like her usual self. Her voice was hard as her nails. She was crouched, poised, knew exactly what to do.

I spun around to face her. She was still pointing the gun at our guests. "Now, both of you. Down on the deck! Right now! Down!" They get down.

"Boops," I say, "What the hell? You are different, somehow."

"Bet your sweet ass, Captain. Now you back off, keep out of this. You are not yet incriminated."

She fished in her ditty bag, plucked out a tiny compressed air police horn and blasted five tweets. Lights burst on all over the jungle. Search lights spotted on us in the boat. On whoever the other guys were, five of them, waiting on the dock. Half a dozen other spots, from the jungle. Two motor launches rounded the bend ahead of us, and one behind, all beamed on us. Fenced in. No place to run, nowhere to hide. The jig, evidently, was busted.

In seconds the launches were tied up to us, and boarded. What? The two Customs guys? They bow to Boopsie and tell her "Nice job, Rios." Then half a dozen more. A launch dropped tenders over the side and our dinghy was surrounded. GeeGee was hands up. He was chattering in espanol, proclaiming, I imagine, that he was innocent. Just a poor peon who was hired to do the heavy lifting. No one listened. They knew who he was.

GeeGee made a dive for it. Splashed head first into the dark water, swimming underneath. One launch brought its spots down on the place. The water was clear as air, very clean for a jungle runoff river. We saw him thrashing, taking off his shoes, wildly trying to swim away. No dice. They were on him as soon as he came up for air. Scooped up like a spawning salmon in bear country. Lucky there were no piranha in this river. Are there? I shuddered thinking about that.

Later, Boopsie introduced herself to me. With a handshake, yet, in her new voice:

"Agent Mirabella Rios, United States Central Intelligence Agency. And yes, I do know how to run the communication equipment."

"Whaaat? You are... undercover... CIA?" I couldn't believe any of this. "I am in some strange nightmare."

This all happened too fast, and too weird, for my simple charter captain's brain to handle. "But, Boopsie, I really like you, the real you. I really, really do. We had something very special going, I thought."

"I know. I like you too, Captain Chuck."

"But, but what is this? It's about this gold smuggling, to redeem a kidnapping hostage? Isn't that - - isn't that what's going down?"

She smirked. Her chirp was back. "This was not what you thought. It's an elaborate scheme, to finance an underground rebellion against the Guatemalan government."

"Ohh...? Ummm ..." As it played out; the only dumb blonde character in this scenario was... *me*.

I stammered, "What about ... Prince Igor?"

"He was also an unfortunate pawn in this much larger game. He took the bait he should not take. He was too greedy to check his facts before he made the deal. He didn't even bother to know where the gold came from. He made a very large mistake."

"So, he has to pay the price? What is that?"

"I do not know. That is not my problem."

"You have a problem?"

"It is not an easy one. It's tricky. Tough."

"Boopsie, I mean, what is your real… Mirabella? I think I am in love with Boopsie. I know I am. With you. I will do anything I can to help you out of your dilemma."

"I appreciate your saying that. You are a good guy. I enjoyed being with you, and I know you were not involved in this plot."

"Could we just stay together after this? I make a decent living in Key Largo with my charter business. You are a wonderful first mate."

She put her fine hands on my chest, reached up to plant a sweet kiss on my lips. "I want to do that. We'll see."

"But your problem?" I am beginning to think like a Captain again. My wits are coming back. My sense of taking command.

"You know I can solve almost any problem on a boat. Maybe I can help. What is it?"

She snuggled her fine blonde head against me, then looked straight up directly into my eyes. I know true love when I see it, and I am crazy about her.

"So," I said, "tell me."

"Getting you out of here, without a scratch."

#

CAPT. CHUCK GNAEGY

Nine

Pirates in Caribbean History

Sir Henry Morgan helped England wrest the Spanish isle of Jamaica from Spain. During England's Dutch and Cuban wars in 1662 he was second in command of Buccaneers in the Caribbean. He made successful raids at Lake Maracaibo in Venezuela; sacked the rich city of Portobello and captured Port Principe. He captured Panama, burnt the city to the ground, and grabbed most of the booty for himself. He had many adventures in the Caribbean; with another base in San Andres, a small isolated island group north of Colombia. At its north end, a tiny island sports a huge, natural bust which looks like him; called Morgan's Bluff. Because the war was essentially over, he was arrested by Nassau Officials and sent to England for trial. But Charles II knighted him instead, and appointed him Governor of Jamaica. The bloodthirsty Pirate lived out his life as a wealthy planter.

The Blue Holes

Deadly Mystery of the Bahama Bank
Pearls of Wisdom from the "Out Islands"

"Down dere, de *Lusca — him of de hands—* he pull you into de lair and you never seen again. De sea crob, he pick you clean. You skeleton, he float down dere. Forevah."

Winthrop Bartholomew, my Bahamian buddy/ guide, would kid you not. He and his people know this legend, this Lusca tale that goes back four hundred years. His brown cheeks and forehead crease with horror as he remembers divers who dared challenge the Blue Holes, and lost.

The Lusca legend was created as far back as the now-native Bahamians can remember. Former slaves whose ancestors, having escaped the sugar cane plantations, settled on this string of tiny cays on the wide Bahama bank. Their simple, almost whimsical stories brand the Lusca as a combination ogre, part shark and part octopus. When a boat or diver dared to defy the curse, its tentacles shot up from the sea and grasped the hapless victims, crew or swimmer. They were dragged down to death, never to return. The Lusca's breathing made the blue holes suck in – outgoing tide – and bubble forth at incoming tides. So that phenomenon becomes reality because of the myriad tunnels and caves. Tides rushing through miles of hidden obstacles wreak havoc and turmoil, they burst through the surface at the holes, while all around, the changing sea may be placid.

In the 1700s, Privateer days, before Woodes Rogers reclaimed Nassau from Blackbeard, it is rumored the Corsairs liked to make unruly captives walk the plank there, for sport; overboard on an outgoing tide, and gleefully watched them disappear in the crystal clear waters. Sucked down into the seas of no return.

Winthrop's eyes rolled into black and white soup spoon ovals. "De boat, big as dis one, de Lusca suck it right in, too. Slurp. Sluuurp. Gulp. Gone forevah.

"De watah comin' out now, bubblin' up outa dere, clear as glass. You see dat now? But den de tide turn, an' de sea rush back in lak a whirlpool. Whoosh. You in dere, bend ovuh and kiss yo sef goodbye. It drink you down like de olive. You gone."

I was standing at the taffrail staring down at a depth I cannot imagine. Blue water, brilliant, ultramarine blue, in a humongous, perfect circle half a hundred yards across. It was nature's huge funnel, the middle of a sparkling turquoise/white bottom plain, a ten foot deep flat stretching 50 miles. But there, in that spot, an endless depth. Boggles the brain stem.

How could this strange thing be out there, in this place? "Out there" is Eleuthra, a far eastern island in the Bahama group. The *Out Islands,* on the edge of a vast plateau.

An infamous Bahama Blue Hole, a round break inthe earth's crust punched by a giant drill bit. A blue puncture in the sea bottom. Drop a superdome into, it would sink out of sight..

This circular tube goes down maybe half a mile, and stretches out into subterranean caverns that may wind ten or twenty miles. It is Mammoth Cave, Carlsbad Caverns, under the Bahama Bank. None have ever been explored to the end. Man's puny equipment does not allow it, just yet. A few tried, and they never came out.

"Help me wit zis dive gear," said my charter, Ziegfried Heffelfinger, a famous underwater photographer who earned his stripes leaping into the kinds of adventures, taking dares, no one in his right mind would entertain. "Vee haf got twenty minutes to a half hour to find out what vee look for in zere."

Sounded like Colonel Klink; I can handle zat;

He chartered my *Sea Diamond* for a week's exploration, in which he hoped to make his indelible mark in science, with photographic evidence discovering the opening and close of a mystery no one had ever seen before. He would author a National Geographix scholarly book on it, he said.

"Geographical theory," Zieg recited, learnedly, "pinpoints zese Bahamas as a thousand mile-long string of emerald green dot islands in the Atlantic Ocean. Zey form 130 million years ago when banks of limestone rose up from za ocean floor. When za last great ice age froze most of the earth's surface, water levels lowered, za banks were exposed. Zen it thaw, refreeze, thaw again, trickles of water seep in to limestone, etch out zinkholes. Za final thaw came, Judgement Day. Zee ocean exploded with new water, rose hundreds of feet, and za caves were submerged, za way zey are now. So, zis is an alien environment. But who are zee aliens here? Vee are."

All around us, spectacular reefs. Not virgin, but pristine, vast areas of golden tube sponges, staghorn coral, gorgonians carpeting the bottom. School fish by the boatload. The bottom paved with miles of graceful staghorns, giant round coral heads. Here a small mountain of coral, 20 feet across, rose off the ocean floor, broken edges, wide gaping holes. Brain coral, star, umbrella corals, green and gold finger sponges, tube vase sponges sprouting from the rocks. But all this was merely an intro to the main event, the vast deep darkness of the giant Blue Hole. We were about to violate its inner sanctum.

I handed him his dive gear. He said, "Put yours on too. You are coming wiz me."

"Just a minute, pal," I said. "You didn't inform me at the start I'd dive in that monster hole. People can get killed in places like that."

"You are carrying my lights. I am za professional photographer. I cannot photograph wizzout lights."

"I am the professional captain, a boat bum, not a diver. I dive when I want lobster for dinner."

"Well, zis time you are going to dive for science. Put it on."

"No dice. That light rack is the clumsiest contraption I've ever seen. Nobs and corners, sharp plastic sticking out all over. Sharp stuff. Like carrying six feet of mounted moose antlers, with searchlights wired on each prong. You are paying me to run a boat here. And that is what I am doing."

He scanned his watch. "You are wasting my time. Vee haf got less than half an hour to dive this hole. I vill double your money. Now put it on!"

"Double?"

"Right."

The arched ceiling of the cave curves outward, down, into a pitch-black pit. The lights throw pale yellow circles onto the walls, picking out brilliant sponges that cling to the rock. Clouds of reef fish sweep past, glittering in the shafts of our 500-watt sealed beams. I gulped as I saw the cavern widen dramatically, downward, plunged into an inky void.

We swam with a strong nylon cord uncoiling, marked every five yards with a numbered flag. Down the face of the wall, the light beams disappeared into pinpoints in the black depths. At 100 feet we saw signs that once this was land, on the surface. Stalagmites. Only a few feet high, not yet the Wizard of Oz, but gaining.

Then suddenly a humongous chamber opened, and all points of reference fell away as though we were in outer space, an Apollo mission. Water so clear we'd see 100 feet, 200 feet in any direction, nothing to point on in the tremendous chamber.

Zieg took a compass bearing, motioned downward. East for two minutes, at 120 feet huge columns, gigantic stalactites strung from an unseen ceiling, like portals in a Roman temple. More than five stories high, in my drop-jawed judgement, ten feet in diameter, solid limestone that had to be millions of years old. They were formed by dripping acidic water over eons of time. I felt a complete load of awesome oozing up my spine.

Zieg was flapping his arms in delight, trying to get

his camera unslung. He motioned for me to hit the lightbutton. I checked my watch. What? We might have ten minutes left.

But we'd have to decompress; down almost 150 feet, the bottom may be 200 or more, and that meant time was running out on us like a faucet.

He was shooting film, but I did not know of what. Nothing was close enough to capture. He was ecstatic, waving his arms and slapping the sides of his head. I wondered if he was a victim of nitrogen narcosis. They get giddy that way. Then finally we turned upward toward the far sunlight.

As we broke the surface, our guide watched, grimly, His darkened features did not reflect the giddiness of Ziegfried Heffelfinger.

"De Lusca, he let you go this time," Winthrop said, "but you look out. You go down der too long, he get you, sure."

On deck, Zieg was all grins. "Zere is a magic to being first," he prattled. "Ven vee turn za lights on down zere, creatures exist that have never seen each other, because zey live in total blackness. Vee opened zere eyes to zere neighbors."

He was no stranger to adventure. In a career of underwater pictures, he had ample opportunity to make the one fatal mistake that says "Za End." He lived through submarine cave exploration, survived more than one shark attack, nitrogen narcosis, handled barracuda and moray eels, photographed dozens of sunken military ships; plunged to the dizzying depths of the Grand Cayman Wall, Cozumel, and Tongue of the Ocean. That's where the 30-foot deep Great Bahama Bank suddenly drops out of sight to a precipitous 1,000 fathoms of choppy blue water. He shot dozens of islands in the Pacific, including the Ghost fleet of Chuuk, the Truk Lagoon, Micronesia, graveyard of Japanese ships sunk by the U.S. Navy in 1944. On one Pacific atoll dive, he discovered a sunken ship that was never found after WWII, in the Marshall Islands, where some of the greatest war battles were fought between the U.S. Navy and the Japanese. He was no amateur, though at times his expertise in boat handling was suspect, and his ego often jumped out in front of his good sense.

Next day, plunging again to 160 feet. Fish in underwater caves, the same as reefs – angels, tangs, parrotfish, grunts, snapper, barracuda, occasional shark. Like desert nomads, continuous migration reef to reef. Moray eels, octopus come to the same digs every night. Put their feet up on the couch?

This time, hugging the limestone wall under clouds of snappers and grunts, a seven foot moray eel, bright neon green, tail curved into a handy coral hole, standing guard over his bailiwick. We saw him yesterday and today. Zieg wanted to go over and scratch his head. As he approached, Mr. Moray squirted straight out, fiery eyes unblinking, mouth full of spiky teeth gaping grotesquely, in full charge mode. Not that cute moray at Key Largo Pennecamp Park that will nimbly snatch a fish out of a diver's mouth; this guy would take your face off. Zieg backed off, chastened but not embarrassed.

Later, deep in the cave our lights picked up an army of bright shining eyes along ledges. Rows of cranberries. Moving in closer, we were startled to see their true origin. On a wide ledge, dozens of gigantic lobsters, fourfeet long, bigger than any I've seen. 20 pounds or more. Lobsters are timid creatures, they quickly learn they're food for predators, and their habit is to hide in the rock outcroppings, under coral heads, in shallow caves. They slink out at night, when predators are foraging elsewhere.

This team was a different league. Not afraid of puny men. These players were so big they marched right out to meet us, waving their long antennae in the current, picking up a scent of ... what? Perhaps looking to sign us up for the menu.

If the spiny lobster had any device other than his carapace, if he had pincers, or claws to inflict damage, these giants could be a threat, so big and aggressive. If a lobster's normal life span is less than a few years, and they shed their outer shells every year, these guys were also very, very mature, very senior for lobster age. A curious thing, these giants, like many other creatures that live at great depths, boasted recessed eyes, rather than stalks like reef lobsters. Must be developed over eons of time. But we were not there for dinner. Theirs or ours.

We moved out. The length of time a man spends in the Blue Hole severely limits observation time; any mistake in dive preparation causes immediate concern. Suddenly too late to not look at your watch. Survival depends on careful prior calculations.

In a cycle of tidal change, not a lot of time left.

We turned into a chamber, narrowed to a slim funnel, face to face with a twelve foot tiger shark.

Sharks over six feet can be a menace, a true risk to

scuba divers, since unless very hungry, a shark is slow to attack another creature as large asitself. A tiger shark is fearless, hulking, aggressive, a torpedo with multiple rows of hooked teeth. This chamber quickly narrowed to a slim funnel barely wide enough for a diver. The gantry crane I carryied wouln't easily wedge through the pass. The shark knew where he wanted to go.

Not likely to give way to a couple of six foot divers. I was jockeying this crazy moose rack of lights and batteries, not moving with my usual ballet grace. I couldn't even back up with a beeper. Big Guy didn't want to. Obviously we wouldn't press our luck with something this large, with all those teeth. Bullies come in all venues. It was accustomed to getting its way.

We had no weapons, stun guns, or double-ought shotgun shell zappers to make this elementary. There to determine what marine life exists and how it is different from normal situations. The tide was on the verge of a head-on rush very soon, no time to second guess.

We stopped, all three of us, in confrontation. Silt knocked from the walls started to cloud our visible spectrum. Water turning milky. We had to make our move. But so did the shark.

Whisked its big tail and came straight at me. All jaws. I tried to slide away, but my clumsy rack scraped the shark's side. A sharp prong caught its gills. It flinched, sweeping its head around. I shoved the light bar at it. The jaws snapped, quick.

Crunch! Spit out the light bulb like a dog tasting broccoli .

Ziegfried also blocked the passage of the 12-footer.

Backed against solid limestone, he was outlined in shadow by the one light I had going. He jerked to face me, fear and loathing in his face mask. Held up his camera to find off the creature. In another second he would be cat chow.

My heart pumped like a Disney cartoon at 10 cells per second. Cramped as it was, I swung the big moose rack, headed for the face of the man-eater, shoved the protruding nobs as close as I could to the gaping jaws. Fanning the switch, I blasted four 500-watt beams into those yellow eyes. If a shark can say "Ach, Schmidt, I give," it did. Whizzed its tail in a snap we could feel and shot out of the tunnel, leaving us to bob in the prop wash.

Hoo boy. Gulp. Now we had scant moments to decompress. Decompression is a *dive now – pay later* proposition. Spend 10 minutes at 180 feet and you have to stop a comparable amount of time at shallow depth – say 15-20 feet – to let the blood components settle down. That keeps you from getting "the bends," nitrogen bubbles in your blood steam. Don't, and that 20 feet can cripple or kill you. The worst part about the bends is that once you get it, you're always vulnerable. So far, we had escaped.

Next day, our last on the Blue Hole, after breakfast, Zeig had a freak slip that somehow dropped a whole sheaf of shot-up negative film, sealed in a flat metal can, over the side. We watched it wafer down, flapping like a leaf from a sycamore tree, until it was caught on the side of the hole, snagged by a little arm of coral. About 60 feet down.

"I cannot get to zat right now, Ziegfried groused .

"I haf got to tally up all zis other stuff and get back to za land so I can write this up." He glancd at me. "Vy don't you just free dive and pick it up?"

"What? Free dive? What am I, a pearl picker?"

"Look, zat is only a few feet down,?" he said. "I am tied up right now, and by the time I am through here, zee tide will start rushing in, and stop any dive program. But if you go right now, it will take you two minutes."

"I am not a pearl picker."

"You are a chicken? You cannot handle this simple thing, like a man?"

"I can handle this. I just don't want to."

"I double your money, again."

"You say double."

"Yez, double, twice." He slid down below to do his books.

There are things I will do for money that I would not do just to save face, or answer a dare. Bravado aside, I also will leap into something stupid once in a while, without measuring the consequences.

I was already dressed in nothing but a pair of cut-offs, for the trip back. The day was beautiful, clear, not a cloud, flat, not a glimmer of wind.

Without a plan, I took three deep breaths and plunged over the side, sans flippers, mask, or artificial lungs. I could see the film can, right down there. Go for a swim. Piece of cake. Tidal suction already pulling downward, it was easy descending into the hole. Reaching the can at about 60 feet, I lifted it off the coral snag, but its handle was tangled in the coral. Seconds lost.

I worked it free, a few more moments. The effort burning my oxygen faster than I intended. But then the can loosened. I leaned back to shove off, my foot tangled in a coral gorgonian. Tripping, I spraddled backward like Saturday Night Live, all arms and legs.

Clutching the can, I fell about 15 more feet before I got my equilibrium, and started to kick, paddle, one-handed upward. Now I felt my breath getting short. I was down more than a minute, and I now had 75 feet to go straight up, against the pull of the tidal current. Neptune, where are you when I need you?

I clawed my way close to the side and began scratching at the wall, tangled with corals and weeds, jerking them out of their nests, using them as a ladder to pull myself up. My skin was pierced by the sharp corals, my elbows were scraped and bruised, my fingertips raw and bleeding as I clawed and grasped at any straw to help me up. And now I heard myself going "U-mm, U-mm, U-mm," as my oxygen was being depleted and I faced "shallow water blackout."

That would put me unconscious without my even knowing it, but it would also kill me. I was now down close three minutes. For a casual diver that is a very long time. I felt my lungs bursting, screaming to take a breath; Take. A. Breath, TakeA-Breath! though there was no air to take in. Only water, and that would kill me.

I was almost to the surface when the black shade slipped down over my eyes, and my unconscious nervous system took over. It would force me to open my lungs and grab for that air. Or else. I gritted my teeth and sealed my lips. The sea closed in around me and I knew it was the end. My last adventure, down the drain. But I would black out and never even know it. Like a boxer, knocked out; he doesn't know it until he wakes up.

Damn. Goodbye, good night, good dammit, world. Cruel sea. Nice ride while ...

Then I felt them. Those *hands*.

The Lusca – him of de hands – those strong hands, latching onto me! I would disappear forever down there and feed the crabs!

Then, as if still in the dream, I was wavering, head spinning with vertigo, waking up, on deck, spewing salt water in wretching coughs. My eyes opened, fluttering. In the strong arms of Winthrop Bartholomew, coughing up enough sea water to float us out of there. His weathered, black, Bahamian face peering at me from a distance of two inches. Squinting into my bleary eyes.

"What ...happened?" I spouted onto his arms.

"De Lusca, he get you, mon. You are dead mon. But I don' let him win. I don' let him have you."

"I believe," I stammered, "in God and the Universe, and now I also believe in the Lusca. Most of all I believe in Winthrop Bartholomew, I owe you one, a very big one."

"I am happy you don' stay down there, Captain. It is not your time."

"What about the film can?" I fumbled with it, snapped open the latch. Looked inside. Nothing. It was empty.

Ziegfried strode up from below. He had missed all the action.

"Hey, Photog," I challenged, "What about this film can? It's empty!"

Zieg colored up, reddish. "Ach, boy. I forget zat. I took it out the film last night and putted the negs to my secure files. Zo zorry about zat."

"Yeah," I said. "Zorry is the right word. Uhm, hey, listen, about the money…"

"I pay you in cash."

"Now."

"Vot you mean, now?"

"I want it now, before I take you back."

He saw I was not joking. He went below, fumbled through his bags, and came up with a thick, fist-full of hundred dollar bills.

I reminded, "You said two doubles.

"Okay. It is all here. Double. Double."

I counted it. All there. A two grand, grand total. I made it in two neat piles on the deck. I picked one up, hefted it, then the other. Then I handed over both to Winthrop Bartholomew.

"I want you to have this money, Win. All of it."

"But, Captain, Why you do that?" His eyes were moist. Mine were, too.

"Because I am alive, here today, and there will be a tomorrow; I give this money to Winthrop Bartholomew…my saving grace…

"Him of de Hands."

\#

Capt. Chuck Gnaegy

Ten

Pirates in Caribbean History

Captain Benjamin Hornigold was a Privateer in theWest Indies, based on New Providence Island (Nassau), another protege' of Blackbeard. He commanded a French sloop from St Vincent in the Grenadines, circa 1713. The pair ravaged many ships up to 1717, one loaded with gold, then split up. When Woodes Rogers came to Nassau to squelch the Pirates' hold on shipping, he commissioned Hornigold to apprehend the Pirates Stede Bonnet and Charlie Vane. Hornigold pursued but lost them both. Later he brought a party of 13 into justice, in a wry twist of circumstance. Hornigold was once considered a founder/stalwart of Caribbean Piracy. Now he had turned into a Marshall; the slight nuance between Privateering and Piracy. Several years later on a voyage to Mexico, Hornigold's ship struck a reef and sank. The fearsome Privateer was never to be heard from again.

Monster of the Green Lagoon

Do not wear it on your shirt.
Snag it with Your Iron Claw

At night, their eyes glow like red hot coals. Like a pair of cherry neon jelly beans floating in a black pool of nothingness.

I was floating in a small skiff off the Intra-Coastal Waterway, right next to the haven where rich men with names like Cornelius Sterling Worth-Gobbs, Vanderbilt, Rockefeller, Morgan etc. laid out huge chunks of money to build "summer cottages" with 17 bathrooms. Some may have called them Industrial Pirates, but the truth was their less than 50 in number of the world's elite, gatherings – giant industry magnates, millionaires, royalty, and old money – could at any given time muster about a quarter of the wealth in the entire world. They called their social club the Golden Isles.

Jekyll island, Georgia.

Two ayem, and I was sweating like a horse that lost its last race, grappling with Dracula vampire mosquitoes the size of pelicans. Waiting to invade the secret hideaway of those brazen scarlet orbs.

There, the monster of the green lagoon lay in wait,

for me, or anything else it could clamp in its jaws. A creepy monster that would slink up in the yard at night to eat your dog, and maybe your kids.

Those eyes, those jaws, no virtual carnivore lusting for computer animated human hors- d'oeuvres, simply trademarks. Genuine flesh and blood descendants of Jurasic Park. One of the most dangerous creatures on mother earth's sweet green planet. A full grown bull alligator, 12 feet long and 800 pounds — may look like nothing more than a sluggish, overblown drainpipe, covered with lumpy rows of olive drab spines and scaly armor.

What it really is, is *Tyrannosaurus Giganticus Rex* with Basset hound legs, built around the most formidable jaws this side of a Great White Shark. In fact, given both the above in the same size, I'm not sure how I'd bet in a free-for-all bite-off.

This is the really bad kid on the block, who grows up to be king of the hill.

This flimsy skiff we were floating in, not even made of steel, was just a vehicle to transport a fly-blown and disgustingly putrid lump of meat, bait, and us, out to where this pre-historic monster could sniff it out, wolf it down, swallow the hook.

At the bow end, I faced backward at my southern good ol' boy guide, who guarded the rear, engine, paddle, and assorted hooks, gaffs, chains, ropes. Tools we may or may not swing to capture or belay the monster.

Between us, in the middle seat, the fragrance of a spoiled pig carcass leaked its guilty secret into the dank night air. I only hoped we'd find out where Big Bull was before he found us. He might decide to snatch off this booby prize, with me practically sitting on it. If you think those blood sucking mosquitoes chomp you, think again. This is no time for a 'scuse me,' or an 'oops.'

I am a simple boat bum, a charter captain more at home on the high seas or a luxury trawler than the Inland Waterway, even if my current ninety-five-foot yachet, tonight, is parked a few hundred yards away. What in God's green slime water was I doing in this fix?

I was volunteered, by a very good friend.

Truth told, I was out on loan, to fill a vacancy created by a compatriot's misfortune. My good friend Leo Spasskey was captain of a rich man's yacht, *Seven Sea Sons*. Based in Newport, it was down for this season to Jekyll Island, which at one time was an exclusive club populated by wallets with more than ten zeros, the richest men in the world. Ol' Spass was now fighting the repercussions of a burst appendix. He languished in the hospital for an undetermined period.

To say a Florida Keys Charter Captain was slightly out of his element is perhaps true, but with a little scrubbing up, I know how to curtsy to these people in the upper crust. I don't do groveling, but I do know how to drive their boat.

What I did not know, and had zip-ah-de-nada experience in, was roping wild animals. I had not ever run down the alley in front of those mad bulls in Pamplona, Spain, and did not often even step in a genuine wild cow pie. I did not know the Loch Ness monster from Adam's off ox, whoever that was.

Now I was looking to perhaps lasso a giant fish, a

ravenous tooth machine. Not the one you name a college after, with cute, sexy cheer leaders and pom-poms. This was the genuine real McGator. Jaws on this —*Tee-Rex*— harbor incisors as long as your forefinger, sharp enough to punch holes in your car door. So large and powerful it could, in one bite, chomp a full grown man in two, right up the middle. Oh, sure, it sports those short little legs, but it can still do up to 30 mph, farther than you can. It can run down a horse, they say, though I don't know by whose authority.

However, my (Spasskey's) employer, in a burst of benevolent gratuitous egotism, volunteered me to organize this operation, "*Get McGator*." The big money lenders in this temple didn't think it was funny having a real live predator stalking in their mangroves. And since I am paid to do what he says, I am in for the duration.

First thing I did was hire a pro. Yes, Virginia, there are pure-fessionals out there who specialize in confronting wild alligators and bending them to their will. The great white hunter I picked was Bronko Hartebeast.

Not only does he know how to do this, he was officially tagged as Alligator Control Specialist by more than one state government. A very large guy himself, full beard, fuller belly dumping over his belt, he could stand in for the 300 lb. countryfied villain on Monday Nite Wrasselin, in Levi's and a big straw hat. Bronk doesn't say a whole lot, but when he opens his mouth the gravelly voice booms out. You'd better listen. If they had mountain men anymore, he'd be one.

"Thet big'un tried to eat me more than once," Bronko mumbled through his beard. He was full of gator stories… like the one about the elderly couple who live on the shores of beautiful Lake Wascagoula. Every afternoon the wife brought her disabled husband out in his wheelchair to watch the sunset, then she'd go back in to fix dinner.

One warm July evening when she came out the second time, a ten foot gator was hunkered there, grinning up at the morsel in the wheelchair, licking its chops. Husband stifled the screams in his throat to a gurgle, didn't make a peep, just tried to keep breathing. Gramma had a table cloth in her hand, and very annoyed, bravely snapped it like a locker room towel. "Out!" She yelled, "Shoo!"

That gator somehow got it that he was persona non-grata. But he didn't sulk or fly into a rage as any rejected house guest might, just turned and shuffled back to Wascagoula. The lake. But not in fear, mind you.

A full grown Bull gator has no fear. Like the 500-lb. Gorilla, it sleeps where it damn pleases. Even if that is in the middle of a $100 million state highway, or a $10 million condo parking lot. Or in your back yard by the canal, next to the greasy barbecue pit.

Would you tell it to leave?

Meanwhile, at the skiff, in the dark water, we were interrupted by a coarse, barking cough. Bronko Hartebeast snapped to attention. Held up a finger. A second later, more coughs. "Thet'll be him," he mumbled. "Comin' in fer us. Ah c'n smell 'im."

He silently dipped his paddle and smoothly whisked us to center of the canal, about 50 yards from the seawall and the tangled mangrove brush on the other side. I felt a shudder of expectancy, or maybe a lizard was crawling up my thigh.

"We'll drap the bait here," he whispered hoarsely. He leaned to pick up one end of the board holding the pig, and it started to slide obligingly toward the black water. But suddenly the bottom of the boat was rammed. The side heaved upward.

"Gol Dangit!" Bronko blurted. "Thet critter's here a'ready! He's tryin' to dump the boat over! Hol' onto the gunnels! She's a rockin!" The boat was humping up and down like a bull bunny in heat, hugely spasmodic. It was a roller coaster ride, ski-run moguls without snow, a bucking bull blast. I was hanging on, feet spread wide and hooked under the seats, white knuckles clutching the sides in a death grip. Gradually it subsided. A wild splash, the gator let us drop back. Undulating waves pulsed, a wake in the narrow canal.

"Hol' on thar!" Bruno ordered. "He'll be back."

For a second it was quiet. We waited. Then a rasping scrape down below, a hard body slam right in the middle of the skiff. It tilted sickeningly up on one edge. The gator's big snout poked out of the water, open-mouthed, rows of hungry, 9-inch nail canines. It whipped to one side, then the other, flinging water at both of us like a fire hose.

I was drenched in a second, so I don't know if I peed my pants just yet, but they were dripping. Make a note: Stop drinking so much beer on these social outings.

Bronko swung the paddle at the gator's nose. It is the only sensitive spot on the entire animal. A sharp whack, another, and the big gator head slid down.

It was quiet for another second. Bronko moved stealthily, rummaging through the pile of equipment on the deck. "What we don't want is for him to get us in the water," he growled. I seconded that. He fumbled in the spilled gear and hauled out a sawed-off .22-magnum rifle, with a pistol grip stock.

"Knowed I might ought ta shoot him," he grumbled, "but not so quick. If'n he dumps this boat over, we get knocked in the water, he'll snap us both in two."

It stayed quiet. Hartebeast laid the pistol across his lap and slipped the paddle out from the pile. Just a few licks and we can be at shore. But Mc 'G' had other ideas. "Watch'im!" Bronko shouted. "Now he's a' top the water."

The big bull gator charged the skiff. Mouth gaping wide open. I swear his head was a yard long, lined up and down with fangs. He rushed in to clamp down on the gunnel. Started to sling it sideways, a dog shaking a rat. The wood gunnel splintered, crunched into woodchips; a live mechanized back yard chipper.

"Geee-zuss!" I shouted, "He just missed my left arm!"

There was suddenly a flash-pop explosion and a simultaneous slapping sound, a zizzz, as the .22-magnum slug hit the bony skull and ricocheted off into the night.

The gator, momentarily stunned, stopped. Released the gunnel. Pulled back. Submerged slowly into the depths.

"Think you killed him?" I offered.

"Hail, no. Thet only jes' gits his attention. Need to get outa heah!" Hartebeast swiped at the putrid pig bait and it oozed over the side, trailing the steel chain and cable. Its distinctive odor clung to the air like a passing garbage truck. Water was pouring through the splintered gunnel. I baled madly with a small bucket.

"Give us a minute, while he smells that," Bronko growled. He whipped out the paddle and dug in. Half a dozen strokes and we were at the shore.

"Git out. Quick!" he ordered, and threw his bulk onto the bank. We hustled the boat onto the rough concrete launching ramp, and sprinted toward his pickup truck. The steel towing cable lay uncoiled on the ground. At its other end, 20 feet of ¾" chain spread on the bottom now, wired to the pig carcass, with a shark hook buried deep inside. Our end of the cable was hooked and wound around a huge winch in the truck bed. We jumped in. Slammed the doors.

I was panting like a marathoner, drenched in canal water and sweat, glad to be alive and breathing. "Is it over?" I gasped.

"Hail no, hain't over!" Hartebeast snapped. "He's still there." "Now we gotta move him onto to the bank."

"But you shot him. Won't he leave us alone now?"

"Don't mean a thang. Thet bullet jes' bounced off'n his skull." He flicked the key and the engine roared. Revved it a couple of times, then reached for the winch switch. Snapped it on, it started to grind, snapped it off. "Jes' checkin.'"

He eased his door open and peered back, surveying the scene. "Still down thar. Eatin' thet pig. If'n he swallers that hook then yep, then we got him."

 We secured the skiff, then checked the cable to the steel drum winch on the truck. That cable would pick up the whole truck if it was but asked. Bronko used it to haul gators up to the bank, to then decide how to dispatch the quarry, or whether. He makes that judgement according to circumstances at the time. Now all we could do is slap mosqitoes. And wait.

 Venture down any waterway, or highway, in Florida at night, or the marshy areas of Georgia, the gulf coast of Louisiana, Mississippi, Texas, and you might see a pair of those of orange-red shining eyes reflected in your headlights. Not like other creatures, whose orbs are bright green, yellow, or white when you light them up. Get close enough, and you can tell which are the big ones; their eyes may be spaced a foot apart. But don't stop. It is the T- Giganticus Rex.

 The American alligator is a 60-million year-old throwback to the Age of Dinosaurs, fitted so perfectly to its environment it challenges even man.

 With supposedly dwindling numbers a few years back, the alligator was classified as an endangered species and protected from being molested, to the tune of five years in jail and up to $5,000 fine. But the gators, belying their golfball size brain, took advantage of a good thing, and multiplied ten times faster than the humans who were encroaching on their natural habitat. There were some bizarre scrapes, and within a few more years the Florida Fresh Water Fish & Game Commission had to establish an alligator control program to protect the populace. It hired professionals, like Bronko Hartebeast, of

West Palm Beach, to remove "nuisance" reptiles.

Not as easy as it sounds. A bull gator also eats whatever it wants. That's where problems come in.

Not far back a 500-pound reptile developed a taste for dog. In one month it ambushed and devoured four full-sized watchdogs along the Hillsboro Canal. The last one was an attack-trained Doberman, leading its master. Like a creature from hell, the big gator burst from the dark water's edge and charged. Within seconds, while the horrified owner watched, the leash still in his hands, the monster lunged with a quick snap of its jaws, swaggered back to the canal and submerged, the squirming dog broadside in its grinning rows of two-inch teeth.

Even more chilling to think about; the Hillsboro Canal runs right across the street from Belle Glade Elementary School, attended by hundreds of children every day. The Fish & Game Commission called in Bronko Hartebeast, professional alligator hunter.

Born perhaps a hundred years too late, Bronko is a replica of the old-time mountain man, one who lived in the outdoors and knew how to handle it; preferred certain aspects of life in the wild over the trials of civilization. In that measure; Bronko may be a lot like his quarry. Steely green eyes, full beard, a bandana tied around his head a la Blackbeard, he carries a foot-long razor-sharp hunting knife strapped to his belt when he's working.

And to him, work means trapping alligators, wild ones; bringing them back alive. Or dead. If he had been born in 1744 he would have been a buffalo skinner, beaver trapper, living wild and free among the grizzly bears. Now, he lives at the outskirts of West Palm Beach.

But he knows his business, just the same.

"Ah larnt about trappin' gators from some good ol' Suth'n boys who taught me everythin' Ah know," he said. "Never had nary a one git away from me yet.

"When they roll in the water, Ah just hol' on and roll with'em."

The 500-pounder, however, was the biggest he'd ever seen, until now. His problem was getting it to the surface, and second, getting a line on to bring it out of the water before loading it into his pickup truck.

"Since them gators lahk ta eat dogs, Ah first lure it to the surface, out'n its den, by barkin' like a dog. Ah also have a tape recordin' of mah old Walker houn', bayin'. Thet works, but when the gator sees me, it'll go back under, and won't come out again."

He'll try other wiles: a baited hook for some gators, a long cable snare for others, and sometimes, his bare hands. Because the 500-pounder was so potentially lethal, he threw out baited shark hooks, loaded with animal suet. It did the trick.

"Ah come back later, and two blocks away heard thet nylon line twangin'. Thet gator rushed agin' it and pulled it up taht like a bowstring. It 'as red-eyed boilin' mad. Ah tied a tow rope and chain on an' trahd to pull the gator up, but the rope broke. Then Ah hooked up the chain -- a three quarter-inch truck tow chain can pull a locomotive— and finally hoisted thet lizard out'a the water.

"Hit landed on the sand writhin' and snappin' its jaws, usin' its tail lahk a scythe. It swung its tail around and caught the other guy at the hip, knocked him right off'n thet bank. Ah knowed then we'd never be able to truss thet thing up, alive. Ever' time Ah come close, it wanted to chomp me."

Hartebeast went to his pickup and unsheathed the .22 Magnum rifle, leveled it, shot the monster clean through the eye. With a brain the size of a golf ball and those hard bony skull plates, that is the only killing shot for an alligator.

The reptile died instantly and Bronko had to call a nearby crane crew to hoist it into his pickup. Back home, he skinned it out and set about collecting his "reward" from the State of Florida. For his services he was allowed to keep the meat— in this case about 100 pounds — which he sold to a local restaurant, Country Joe's. The 100-pound hide went to the state where it was auctioned off at the Capital, in Tallahassee. Hartebeast received 70% of the gross price.

Hartebeast minimizes the income he gets from gator hunting, as well as the dangers, calling it a "hobby sorta thang." But like all men who, at times, live on the edge of certain death, his reward is as much the pumping of adrenaline, the high of a thrilling contest and conquest, as the money. One suspects he would really enjoy wrestling one of those 11-foot monsters under water, just like in the old Tarzan movies. With the smaller gators, five or six footers, he sometimes does just that.

"When they bite, they roll," He said. "It's easier in the water, because the resistance of the water keeps the gator from smackin' you with its tail. Ah do it in shalla' water where Ah kin stand if Ah have to. No Tarzan act. But Ah do carry a knife, in case a gator gits aholt a me'n drags me to deep water. Ah'd try to cut the spinal column in back of its head.

"The best way is to get a line on 'em with a catch stick. Then Ah jump right on its back and put my knees behind its front legs. They usually got the mouth open so Ah take my hand and smack its nose, hard, and it shuts its mouth. Ah reach around and holt its mouth shut and pull its head back, all the way back in a big curve, tight, and wind some tape around its mouth. Then Ah grab the legs and tie them up, like bulldoggin' a steer, and load the gator into the truck. Sometimes Ah might git three in one night."

Each alligator is individual, Hartebeast points out, so he must proceed with caution every time. Once in a while he finds an easy one, like the eight-footer reported sleeping in the parking lot of a fashionable condominium.

"A man come to git in his car and the gator was lyin' right a'side it, asleep. The old gent was rilly scart, so they called me. The gator never did get aggressive. Ah jes tied its feet, taped its mouth, picked it up like a pet dog, and loaded it in the pickup. No sweat."

A big bull alligator is a traveler, Bronko told me, and will travel an area of 30 or 40 square miles. if that territory includes populated places, the gator doesn't mind. After being born about six inches long, and having enemies such as the black bass and Everglades hawks to worry about, it is protected by its mother for about the first year. After that, the gator is a couple of feet long, and like the grizzly bear, is the bully kid on the block. Nothing messes with it. By the time it's six feet, big as a man, it outswims any fish or aquatic animal, runs 30 miles per hour on land in short bursts; will eat anything in sight. Bronko finds cans, bones, sticks, rocks, whatever captures their fancy, in their stomachs.

This one was not that different. It was now 4 a.m., and suddenly we heard a little creak, a shuffle. The cable began to slide on the rocky bank. McGator had taken that huge chunk of bait. Moving a little faster now.

Bronko set the truck's handbrake. Checked the cable winding on the drum, clicked the switch. The big drum, taking up slack an inch at a time. Minutes dragged on. The winch ground slowly, until finally the cable picked up off the ground. Then it pinged snug.

"Now we see what we got," Bronko said under his breath.

The cable twanged, tight. Groaned. Then stopped. The winch shuddered. Stopped.

"Ain't pickin him up," Bronko said. "Caught on a rock, maybe." He climbed into the truck. Revved the engine. The winch tried again. Picked up a couple of inches. We began to smell it overheating. "Ain't pickin him up," Bronko growled again.

Slowly, the truck started to move. Inching backward. Tires sliding. The gator pulling it backward toward the water. Bronko was livid. Veins stood out on his neck. He climbed in the truck, revved the engine. "Ye ain't gonna win this'n, gator! Ye ain't gonna win!"

He took off the handbrake and revved the engine. Put it in low-low gear. Eased on the accelerator. Revs going higher. The motor loud and complaining. Bronko took his foot off the gas, let the cable go slack. It started to move backward again. He jammed his foot on the gas.

The cable twanged tight. He goosed it. Moved the wheels a foot or two.

"We gonna win this, gator!" he shouted into that dark and dangerous night.

The cable moved again, the wheels rolled half a turn, slowly. Then the line went slack. The tires caught and the truck spurted forward four feet before it stopped again. Then another five feet. "He's a'comin' out!" Bronko shouted.

He jumped out of the truck, .22-magnum in hand. "Now, you git in that truck and keep pullin' till he comes ashore. Y'heah?"

I climbed in. The truck was still inching forward. I gunned it, and the cable came tight again. Then it slackened.

"Stop it there!" Bronko yelled. "Come on out here and do it with the winch. We gonna git this gator now."

But suddenly, the gator was on the launching ramp. Swaggering, marching footstep after footstep, out of the water, dragging the cable behind. To end this waltz of the toreadors in its own way.

Huge. Three feet wide or more. Its head looked the size of a Volkswagon bug. And it was mad as hell. Deliberately marching right at us.

Bronko raised the sawed-off .22. Then stopped, fumbled in his pocket. "I'm out'a ammo!" he blurted. "In the glove compartment! Git me thet box! Quick now!"

I rushed to the truck. Fumbled in the glove box. It was in the back. I clawed after it, and finally grabbed the brass-filled ammo box. Then I heard Bronko yell.

The gator had backed him up onto the truck bed,

and was trying to raise itself up. Bronko was smacking it on the nose with a big shovel. Every time it lunged at him, he'd haul off and smack it. "Gimme that ammo!" he yelled.

I had to run around the other side and climb up. I shoved the ammo box at him. He whacked the gator's nose one more time and it dropped to the ground.

Bronko grabbed a long magnum cartridge and shoved it into the breach. "Now, you sucker, rise up here jes' one more time!" He braced himself, both hands on the gun, aiming deliberately at the monster's big right eye.

The rabid gator was not afraid; monstrous, vicious. It reared up, 4-inch-long teeth crunching, snapping, roaring. Lunging to grasp Bronko's legs. Trying to rip Bronko in two. Instead, it missed, grabbed the winch drum and clamped down hard. Teeth scraping against metal, as it locked on.

Bronko pulled the trigger.

It is certain that Bronko Hartebeast, before he retires, will have plenty of of bed-time chronicles to thrill his grandchildren.

There's the one about the blind, three-legged gator he captured on a high bridge over the Intra-Coastal Waterway ... the one where a man bitterly criticized him for gator trapping as cruelty; then called a week later, crying; a big one had gobbled up his pet poodle... the one that tried to snatch a $5,000 pony...

#

Capt. Chuck Gnaegy

Eleven

Pirates in the Caribbean History

Stede Bonnet, the "Gentleman Pirate" was a wealthy, educated New York land owner when he met Edward Teach, aka Blackbeard. Teach invited Bonnet, and his ship Revenge, to sail alongside the Pirate's Queen Anne's Revenge. Soon Blackbeard realized Bonnet was not the reckless Pirate leader he had expected. In 1717 he forced Bonnet aboard his Queen Anne and put another Pirate in charge of Bonnet's galley. As new prizes were won their fleet quickly became four, with a contingent of 300 Pirates, causing a high seas nightmare of pillage and terror from the Caribbean as far north as Maine. When they reached the Royal Fleet's blockade at Beaufort Inlet, N. Carolina, the rogues lost two vessels; one the Queen Anne's Revenge. Blackbeard seized a smaller sloop, Adventure, and escaped with most of the loot. In 1718, Stede Bonnet and his crew were apprehended, then found guilty and hanged, at Wilmington, North Carolina.

Survive the Savage Sea

Dye Marks the Spot

I was single handing, from the enchanted little party-rock island of Margarita, just off the Caribbean coast of Caracas, Venezuela. Bound for San Juan, Puerto Rico. I spent some quality time with my good friend Captain Horatio Kernblower there on his big shrimp trawler. I couldn't know then how similar our fates would turn out. We brought giggles at all the little cafes and clubs with our broken espanol, and bought and sold genuine Rolex watches, which you can pick up cheap in any Margarita bazaar for $35. And you can't help thinking while they are most likely not real gold, you bet, they do keep time, plus you can impress all your friends you have not sold one to yet.

We also did a tourist flake and flew in a four-seater over famous Angel Falls. Highest in the world. Which from the top, since it was the dry season, now looked more like some hip local teenager was hiding up there in the rocks with a fire hose, shooting it off the cliff to drop half a mile, taller than Victoria, or Niagara. Keeps the touristas coming, and they happily return year after year to marvel.

But now here I was solo, with about 800 miles to go, and the third day out dawned not clear, with roiling seas and winds. Maybe 18 knots to start, steep punchy rollers. I was on a broad reach in my *Pagan*, 43-foot custom sloop-rigged motor-sailer. No engine thrumming, just sliding up and down those five footers with a wind-assist. I was propped up comfy in the deckhouse, bare-foot, with toast, orange marmalade and coffee.

Morning radio net said watch out, we're gonna get some. Something. First tropical pina-colada whiplash this season. Tropical wave. No nasty problema, I thought, it was not yet even June. Nothing to cringe in the lazarette about for a couple more months. April Fools Day, my favorite holiday.

Still, I ran down my gear check again. Did a slow walk around the deck, engine room, through-hulls. Took a turn on anything that closes. Outside Caracas I had hauled the boat, got a bottom job; it sparkled like blue petroleum jelly. All secure. I was so proud.

On a broad reach, about six knots. Easy rider. Now that's class. But as my long day's jouney into paradise wore on, I was alone, and a touch lonely. I missed my latest honey who dumped me – gee, how long ago was that? They are all looking for a millionaire. Me, too.

I wasn't yet beginning to eye that full size plastic blow-up doll those jokers gave me as a bon-voyage. They trussed her up when I wasn't looking. She's still up there, spread-eagled in the rigging, across the yard arm. Tied hand and foot. Stark naked. Such a nice smile she has. So Inviting. I left her there for all to see, but nobody passed yet to take a quick shot at my prize. So far not even the male seagulls are interested.

My *Pagan* handled these lumpy seas like a champ. By later afternoon I checked my heading and position. All fine. A little wine with din-din, Chilean red goodie grog, and before I knew it, ready for some bunk time.

I nap upstairs, in the deckhouse when I am single handing. Seems to keep me alert. Rely on my ESP or intuition to warn me of any traffic. I switched on the big diesel and let it go just past idle, in gear. I was clever enough not to be in the sea lanes, so all should be okay. I waken every hour or so, then nap out again.

Not my first time. Wind was still pumping up, but *Pagan* rode soft and sure, a nice, fat marshmallow. Rocked me to paradise. I felt my eyelids start to get heavy. I dozed off in the deckhouse.

Aaaarrggh. What? Three a.m.? I did more than doze off. But something…strange. *Pagan* was wallowing, not crisp, and when a big wave hit her, on the starboard quarter, the splash went high up across the big side windows. Where was I, in a tenement basement?

Instantly alert. What is happening here? Up, and staggering from the gyrations of the boat. A big wave slapped us sideways, and the boat answered with a matronly roll through it, then righted herself. I heard… water? Gurgling?

From the deckhouse, it was three steps down into the galley, then two more to the staterooms. I made the first three okay, but when my bare feet touched the polished teak parquet deck tiles, my foot slid. Wet! More than that. Ankle deep wet!

I snapped on the 12-volt lights. Water! Water, on the lower deck, several inches. What the...

I moved quickly to the steps down to the stateroom. Solid water! Knee deep already. I forced open the latticed door, saw water, two, three feet deep in the stateroom. We were definitely in deep trouble.

My brain box rattled: Coast Guard, where are you when I need you? No dopers on this route; you're all out chasing go-fast smugglers.

Get the life raft ready? What about provisions? Water? Where's it coming from? How can I stop this? Could I stop it? Must be a cause. Find it! Find the damned leak!

I was wrestling up floor hatch covers when the lights first flickered. Water up to the batteries, below in the engine room. Time slipping away, down the drain. Hull must be a quarter full already. I grabbed a flashlight and tried to shine it down through the hatch to the bilge. Black. Oily. Paper towels, provisions floating, swirling around. What? My bilges are always clean. What is this? I could see nothing down there to give me a clue.

I popped open up the big steel hatch covers on the engine room. Still running like Ferrari-Andretti, sloshing, spraying buckets of water as the wheels spun. Bilge pumps running all out, but on the losing end. Shone the flash down there; all dark water. Black. Olive oil. No way to see where it's coming from. Shaft seals? Broken thru-hull fitting?

If so, how could I find it? Couldn't see a damned thing in that dark pool. No current stream to tell me which direction to look. Water constantly shifted as the boat rolled. No way to find out. Pawed down through the oily liquid. Feel-checked every thru-hull. All secure.

To put this much water in there in a few hours, it must be a big break. The head?

The one place I cannot check the valves, under the deck and jammed into a corner under the shower. The head. I didn't design this boat. If I stretched out on my belly, if I could hold my breath for 5 minutes, perhaps I could reach through… won't happen. No way to get there. Fiberglassed in. If I had time, I could chop or saw my way through the shower compartment floor. It was already inches deep underwater. No way to get there.

I struggled up, out on deck. Wind was still picking up, perhaps heading for the forecast light gale, 15-20-30 knots, but not dangerous in itself. Yet.

Think! You bozo. Find a way out!

Tried the radio. VHF Blank. Zilch. "Hey! Anybody out there? Any boat hear me?" Out. Water shorted it out. No way to communicate. The last resort, the EPIRB. Not ready for that yet. Have to try everything; save my ship. Up on deck. Wind was singing in the lines and stanchions. Seas were lumping, rushing the starboard quarter, crashing against the hull. Galloping away. Would it change anything to go stern to? Bow to? This was already the most likely best angle.

Pagan was making way, it seemed, and could be on the course that was set up before this started. No advantage to change it now. Couldn't you wait till morning light? Come on, Saturn!

Back down below. I couldn't stop the inflow. Couldn't even see where it's coming in. It was getting worse by the minute. What now? Now what?

Only One answer. I dreaded it behind my eyes. There was no choice. Only one.

Get out. This is no drill. My lovely *Pagan* was going down, to hell, in a coco palm-frond basket.

Had to get ready. How the hell do you get ready to leave your boat, your life, in the middle of a storm? Four hundred miles from land? If you did not … what is the alternative? You are not the Captain of the Titanic. No pride, no heroism involved here. Only your whole life. Nobody will take your picture or give you a medal or slap a bouquet of flowers on your grave. Uh-ugghh.

Suddenly I remembered Geoff, the young guy who was learning scuba diving and sailing in Key Largo, mate on a fishing boat, dive boat. Whatever would take him out on the water. Loved it. One day they asked him to help sink a small sailboat for the artificial reef. No big freighter, which takes a crew of ten or so, just a couple of guys, guide the operation, make sure it went where they wanted to hit bottom. On the sand, not the reef.

Geoff was eager to go, to get the hours and opportunity to see how it was done. Out in 125 feet of water, just past the shallow reef line; everything ready. Kid standing on deck forward of the hatch, at the bow in full scuba gear, mask on, figuring the boat would settle straight down. He'd ride the sinking bronco. No problem. What fun!

But when the plugs were all pulled, a small explosion down below to open a big gash, the boat heaved down bow first. Tipped down and headed for the bottom. Geoff was slammed backward, smacked down into the forward hatch, his mouthpiece and mask were torn away. The rush of water over the boat pinned him inside. No escape.

The boat plunged straight down to 125 feet. Pinned inside, Geoff fought to get loose, escape, but couldn't. His ear drums were imploded, he was coughing blood, disoriented, groping, trying to locate his scuba mouthpiece, find his way out.

They dove for him within minutes, but a lot of damage was already done. Alive, but four weeks in and out of the hospital. Dizzy, Disoriented. Vertigo. Joint aches and pains. He would never dive another time. He went back to Wisconsin and I never heard from him again. The thought rushed at me. I hope is he is okay. But the lesson never left.

Where did that leave me? In several thousand feet of water. The Puerto Rican Trench goes down to 27,000 feet. If my *Pagan* went for the big plunge, I wanted to be as far away from it as I could get. Nobody around to fish me out, damaged or otherwise. And, gulp, nobody swims back from 27,000 feet, or however far it is down there.

That course I took on water safety. What did it say? Yeah, wear a life jacket, stay out of the water, climb on debris, drink a quart of water a day, eat carbo bars, drop a dye marker if you see a rescue boat or plane, shoot a flare, don't panic. Don't Panic?

My whole world was about to tip its nose down and reach for the bottom, and they tell me do not panic. Water was closer now; would soon rush over the deckhouse floor.

Okay. Okay. Dinghy. Dinghy. I always made a list

before every voyage. Survival 101, I called it, but never expected or intended to use it for real. Pack the dinghy with supplies, water, fishing gear, life vests, EPIRB. I struggled to my chart desk and pulled out log books, boat papers, charts, radio, binocs, flares. Sweat dripping down my armpits. Heavy breathing. Was that wetness on my face angry tears? Could this be happening?

What else was in that course? Oh yeah. The primary goal is to be picked up, soon as possible; not to spend six weeks at sea in a life raft, or on a packing case. Even though I read of the guy who, they say, lasted 300 days on a hatch cover, living on rain water and fish, before they picked him up. But if you are not picked up, they advise, you have to handle emergency situations as they come. Good boatsmanship, I say. Gee, thanks.

The ocean doesn't give a damn who you are. The Sea is not your friend. It treats everybody the same, like a single coconut that falls off the tree into the surf at Tahiti. Its survival and delivery to a supermarket in Los Angeles is strictly up to its own preparation. Hey, where am I, is this Miami Beach or Nova Scotia?

Even then, if they come to get you, it is not easy in mountainous waves and high winds, to climb into a helichopper basket.

The sooner you are picked up, the better your chance of survival. That's where the EPIRB comes in (Emergency Position Indicating Rescue Beacon).

I pulled on foul weather gear and worked my way out on deck. Wind was up even more. Concentrate. Zero in on the one thing you have to do right now, and do it. Then the next thing. Seas tossing us, but with *Pagan* full of sea water we were sloshing, wallowing between waves. They'd splat and wash over. One of the wide ports on the deckhouse was suddenly crashed in by a roller. Water poured inside. I hated to see it, but soon enough, that was a moot point.

The lights went out. Now it was darkness and wind noise, rolling deck and no way to keep balance. I became aware of the wind noise; singing in the shrouds. No siren's song.

Brutal chords, mismatched. The ship was so erratic in her movements I couldn't stabilize myself. I worked my way to the dinghy, it was on the lee side.

I tore off the cover, unbuckled the harness –in a dream state – and pulled the halyard that lifted her free. The little beast was poised there, arms open for me. I was suddenly knocked down by a wave that shot up over the deckhouse. We were now so low in the water. I grabbed another flashlight, stowed and secured my plastic bag full of papers and gear. No other way out. Staggering with the roll and wind.

I hauled on the halyard that lifts the dinghy. Didn't take much for her to clear, the top deck was now awash. It was a matter of seconds. I climbed aboard, heaved on the halyard and she was free. I let the line run as we were scooped up by a new, crashing sea. A sudden stop. Thrown suddenly sideways.

The halyard, running out, jammed in the block. We veered violently, pulling the ship towards us, us toward the ship. We were tethered. She would pull us down with her. I did not lust for her company anymore. I clawed out my Bowie knife and slashed at the heavy halyard.

Couple of swipes, sawing, the line parted. The dinghy, with me spread eagled on both gunnels to steady her, moved downwind, skittering, wallowing away from *Pagan*.

Okay, Captain Ahab, What is your next move?

EPIRB. I fastened its tether securely to a seat plank; clicked the activation switch. The light on top blinked on, a yellow glow reflected on my yellow rain gear. I couldn't hear it chirping but I knew (hoped) the radio message was bleating out to satellites. Someone, anyone, hearing it would, I prayed, pick it up, pluck me from the ravenous storm.

Pagan took another roiling, rolling half hour to make her exit dive. I was staring intently into the gloom able to just make out her silhouette through the driving storm. A grey-white ghost hull, singular, alone, forlorn, her darkest hour. I loved her still.

The plastic blow-up sex doll still clung to the yard arm, smiling that exotic smile, her legs flying free, an invitation I could not bring myself to recognize. I glanced down at my watch only a second, 05:38. Looking back up, *Pagan* gave up the ghost. slipped away.

She was gone.

I was dumbfounded. Speechless. Were those tears coursing down my face? I sincerely hoped so. Does a full grown sea captain bawl? Or was that terror whipped by the wind and rain? Now an hour before dawn I was half way between Puerto Rico and Venezuela, 400 miles from any land, alone in a 12-foot dinghy on the wild, churning sea.

I sank down into the shallow depths of the little

boat, snapped the tarp from one gunnel to the other, on my back, and closed my eyes. Just hang on. Hang on. It's too goddammed late to cry.

I didn't sleep, but wished I could. Darkness wasn't quite complete; the low clouds were not totally black and the roiling sea's breaking waves rushed past, hung, exploded into spray, and gathered for the next roller coaster. Following, building, chasing, catching up, bursting, flinging spray to the sky, then going black again to gather the next performance. The entire scenario rerpeated over and over behind my eyes, endlessly, like a loop on a DVD, CD Rom, play through, play again, play again.

Just at dawn, the sky slowly turned grey and roily, no low clouds, stringy mist.

The front had passed. Seas still lumping, charging, rushing on like a herd of white buffalo. I heard it, far above, a jet. It passed almost directly overhead, but kept traveling east into the lightening sky. Perhaps Mexico City to London, I surmised. Then, in a wide circle, it banked and turned, toward me. Circling, losing altitude. Was it trying to locate my EPIRB? I prayed.

Yes. Yes! It was down to 2,000 feet, easing down. I saw, a Coast Guard jet!

I rose half way sitting up, waved. Of course they could not see me yet. But they were homing in. I fumbled with the dye marker, dropped it over the side, and immediately a huge circle of yellow spread, even in this confused sea. It must have covered 60 yards or more, before the jet throttled back, descending more rapidly to less than 500 feet. Easing down. With a direct bearing on me. On my EPIRB. But they saw my dye-marked circle.

I watched the tiny package leave the plane and sail downward on a small parachute with a long ribbon attached. The way they estimated the winds and current was exacting. That tiny parachute hit the water no more than 200 feet away, up wind, the long ribbon trailing out so that it drifted right across my dye marker, almost exactly to me. Bingo, USCG! I grabbed the ribbon and hauled in the package. It was a radio.

I snatched it up, punched the 'talk' button. "Hey, thanks, guys. Thanks. Am I glad to see you! Thanks. I thought I was a goner down here."

"This is Captain Jim Fellows," he answered. "We have your exact coordinates, your EPIRB did the job it was supposed to."

"Roger that, Sir. I am – was – Captain of the *Pagan,* 43-foot motor-sailer that went down a couple of hours ago. How do I get out of this?"

"We can't land, of course, and you are just out of range of our choppers. So you'll have to wait until somebody comes by. We've located a Japanese fishing trawler about 25 miles away. He'll come pick you up. It'll be a couple of hours. Are you okay?"

"Roger. Good shape."

"Anyone on there with you?"

"Nary a soul. Lucky for them, huh."

"Okay, Captain, he will be coming by soon. In the meantime, rest easy."

"Roger that."

The jet circled again, dipped its wings, and rocketed off to the northwest.

Two hours later, on schedule, the fishing boat

Osaka Maru hove into view. A big fishing boat, 85 feet long, black hull. It dropped a cargo basket and net over the side. I crammed everything I had in there and climbed aboard.

"I Captain Yoshiro Matsazumi," he said, sing-songy. "You have time to go with us?"

"Uh, yeah, guess I have time to do whatever you want. You picked me up."

"That good. We fish."

In the days that followed, I thought again about Kearnblower's saga, learning more about long-line deep sea trawl fishing than he ever wanted to know. But at the end of the week, Matsazumi delivered his cargo to the fishing port in Trinidad, and was thanked profusely for his hospitality, which included all the raw fish I might savor for those four days. That's what his crew eats, every day, every meal.

They catch a hundred fish, skin four or five out then and there and have dinner. Raw, almost still throbbing. Ah, so.

Those Nipponese know what they like.

So, I invited him to call me if he is ever in Key Largo so I can take him out to dinner. I owed him one very large one. A steak. Well done, rare, or raw. His choice.

From Trinidad it was a short haul to the airport and return to the States.

I reflected on my last voyage on *Pagan*. I knew it might take a while and some haggling to bludgeon the insurance company into replacing her. They were sure to insist that somehow it was my fault, negligence, poor record keeping, perhaps a deliberate oversight that let all that water in. Act of God: that lets them out of every scrape.

There are times, sure, I wonder, and study, and question, but nothing ever quite jells for me explaining exactly what happened to my *Pagan* that night. My beloved *Pagan*. If I could, I'd find out everything and put it in my diary, my log, so it can never happen again. But that is, of course, only guesswork.

So, what was it all about?

What fine lesson did I learn from this great adventure? Well, maybe this…

Key Largo Boat Captains do not eat sushi.

#

CAPT. CHUCK GNAEGY

Twelve

Pirates in Caribbean History

Perhaps history's most notorious Pirate was Captain William Kidd, whose treasure at least in part, was salvaged on Gardiners Island, off New York's Long Island. He held a Royal Commission as an English Privateer against the French in the West Indies, deep in the Caribbean, in 1696. His ship, the Adventure Galley, also sailed the African coast in search of quarry, but found none. So he turned to Piracy. With minimal success, his crew close to mutiny, the swashbuckler captured an Armenican Merchant off Hispaniola, then bought a new ship, Antonio, and sailed for New York. Governor Earl Bellomont charged him for Piracy, sent him to England for trial on five indictments. Kidd was sentenced to hang, at the Thames in 1701. His body, encased in a gibbet (cage/gallows), was displayed in London's public square as a warning against piracy. His ghost, they say, returned many times to protest his innocence, and vow his revenge.

Dive to Paradise Atlantis & Beyond

Ancient Pyramids, the Bimini Road

I was Staring down into the clear, lemon-lime jello thirty feet deep, into the long ago past, I could feel the vibration off Paradise Point. The millennium past. Ten thousand years ago, an advanced civilization thrived on this spot. Before pirates, pearl divers, automobiles and A/C, moonshots and international space stations; before anything we might understand about who or what came before.

My breath was quick and light; someone was sending me a subliminal message. ESP? Could I believe that? The sender was a doctor of philosophy, PhD, a professor at several substantial universities, a man noted world wide for the depths of his insights into ancient behavior. So, was I an ancient in this study?

His thoughts crept into my wetsuit; I felt them telling me I had lived here before, as he did also, with perhaps a million other people. There were all the modern advantages, plus a special talent that had not dropped down through the ages.

Not just walking erect or indoor plumbing and alternating current. We, he maintained, had the ability to communicate by mind alone; and we may have been descendants of extra-terrestrials. That, in a nutshell, explained our mission here, together. Part of our destiny was to find each other, in some way. We were somehow connected by a force we could not deny.

The idea seemed reasonable when he explained it. Why else would we have met?

No need to talk? I wasn't sure I understood; so how would you tell someone they have a piece of left-over spinach stuck on a front eye-tooth?

He dismissed insignificant items. Spinach was not the object of this revelation. The subject, and the predicate, and object was...

Atlantis. The place we were looking down on, right there, was ancient Atlantis, he insisted. And since he had studied primordial civilizations with years of expertise — more than I could ever imagine – how could I doubt his ideas? How this marvel came to pass...

I was relaxing on my steel trawler, *Write Stuff,* on a ripe evening in June. The moon was blue and I was too, reminiscing about the true love of my life who flounced out, left me high and dry on a shoal. Because we were no longer in St. Thomas or St. Barts; and I wouldn't take her to the Dolphin Ball at the Edgewater Hotel in funky ol' Key Largo. One reason, I'm only a charter boat captain, I do not own a pair of sox. Could I go to a Dolphin Ball wearing cut-offs and boat shoes without sox?

There was a knock on my transom. Ha! She'd come

crawling back to me! Her sexy charter boat captain without a sock to dance in.

But it wasn't her. It was a tall, slender, grey-haired man who must have been the model for those college professors or CEOs they use in TV ads.

"Marston Valentino Jones," he said. "I understand you know everything about navigating the Caribbean, and the Bahama Islands."

"Well, that's stretching it," I admitted, "but yes, I've sailed in the Bahamas. I know what to look for, and where to see it. You are a fisher person?" (Notice how I am adapted to the non-gender designations now considered non-offensive to anyone, even if they are also non-descriptive. I am afraid our language is in trouble from non-specificity).

"I am an archaeologist," he said. Researching ancient civilizations."

"Jones? Archaeologist? You are the real, honest to goodness Indiana Jones?" I vaulted over the taffrail. "I am so happy to meet you, sir. I have seen all your movies!"

"I am not Indiana Jones."

"Oh. Well, that's okay. I am not Amerigo Vespucci, either. I am just a simple boat captain. What might I do for you today, sir?"

"I want to charter your boat for a trip to Bimini, and possibly other fertile sites."

Fertile? I knew the population of Bimini was more or less stable for a couple of hundred years, the reason being a lot of young people migrate to Miami. Surely it wasn't a den of fertility rites. "Whatever you say, Doctor

Jones. Uhm—what will we do there?"

"We are going to explore probabilities that may lead to a breakthrough in our knowledge of links to the ancient past."

"Ohhh. Well, that is exciting, to say the least." I had never considered links of that sort in my wildest dreams. The farthest ancient past I knew in my life was my grandmother, who loved me in spite of myself.

"When can you be ready to embark?"

"I'm ready when you are, Indy, er… Dr. Jones."

In the days that followed, I got to know Professor Jones. He was a very nice man. A true gentleman. A brilliant student who arrived at his theories through exhaustive studies. He was a Yale PhD, a world renowned expert in paleontology, archaeology, zoology, geology, and a hallowed member of the League of International Explorers. A genuine, super heavyweight. Awesome.

Author, lecturer, talented artist, here was the 800-lb. Gorilla in a world of naïvete, undereducated riff-raff like… yours truly. I felt, when I heard him speak about the intricacies of life, the eons that passed before us, that he would be the one guru I'd climb a mountain to sit at the feet of. Even in the classroom, if they might allow me in there.

But… Atlantis? It seemed this discovery happened in a roundabout way, not necessarily in line with his other accomplishments. A fisherman had discovered an intricately carved granite column lying underwater in the Bahamas, some years back. He brought that strange, foreign stone to a scientist he knew was interested in archaeology – Dr. Jones – who was immediately fascinated by further implications, however implausable.

That discovery changed the course of his life. No less. Although he studied evolutionary theory and the origins of ancient civilizations all his life, this opened to a whole new calendar of possibilities. It lit his fire to search out more evidence of Atlantis, which, he said, resulted in spectacular underwater archaeological discoveries.

What were they?

Pyramids on the ocean floor, megalithic ceremonial shrines, mysterious lost cities, baffling tales of extraterrestrials – I am not making this up – all led Dr. "J" into a bizarre maze of science and para-science. Along the way, he collaborated in several best-selling books on Atlantis and the Bermuda Triangle, and proposed theories which other men of pure science criticized as unacceptable. And so, with his brilliant scientific mind, even though he had found a chunk of the Holy Grail, all was not peaches and CoolWhip. He was ostracized by his colleagues.

Later, now at the site, we strapped on tanks and dive gear. One thousand yards off the beach at North Bimini, due north of the old Rockwell mansion on a point. We were there to dive the most exciting piece of actual evidence, he said, that Atlantis existed. In three fathoms of water off the northwest coast of Bimini, a strange construction called the "Bimini Road."

He found this, at first unbelieving, like a bolt out of the blue. Definitely a predestined chapter in his life, he was certain. On that particular day he was looking for a storied pinnacle, or pyramid, which rises up about 3,000 feet from the ocean floor in the Gulf Stream. It came within 60 feet of the surface and was a mile long. Fate turned them down.

They could not locate this fabled high-point, and instead of investigating further, Dr. "J" asked his guide – Bonefish Sam, famous for guiding Ernest Hemingway – about a shallow reef, a place to relax, dive and collect a few tropical fish.

Sam said, "Sure."

"By Jupiter," Dr. Jones told me, "There was my answer."

I was over the side first, to check that my anchor was secure, and no predators prowled my dive site to endanger my client. Forever safety conscious. But what was this?

Through the crystal clear ocean, thirty feet deep, I was looking at the remains of a… building? A foundation? Huge, awesome megalithic blocks of stone, cut in squares and rectangles, all fit together side by side, measured width, though some of the stone corners were rounded by many eons, centuries of sea erosion. It trailed off into infinity. But the geometrically precise positioning showed it had to be a remarkable engineering feat. Built by people who knew highway construction. Not a freak of Mother nature.

I swam along, wondering — How big is this? How Long? Where did it go? And finally: Why was it there? The answers were not easily figured. The "road" angled away from the beach contour, arrow-like, for about 2,000 feet, then it made an exact 90 degree turn for another 328 feet, then turned again to form a U-shape. Or rather, a deep J-shape. Hmmm, "J", for "Jones"?

The stones are flint-hard micrite, Dr."J" told me later, they are not soft beach rock, and actually ring when smacked with an iron sledge hammer. The huge slabs, big as a living room 16 to 20 feet square, and two to four feet thick, were uniform, flat on the top surface, and set side by side. I could not have any idea how heavy they were, who put them there, or how they did it. But it was not beach shale.

One of the most telling facts about this structure, he told me, was that 10,000 years ago this entire Bahamas area was several hundred feet above water!

So the debunkers who later claimed this was merely beach rock, had not considered the earth's evolution, and apparently had not seen for themselves.

Along the "road" farther down is a series of smaller stone sets, three by five feet, also hewn and fitted to a pattern, not random. The smaller stones are set in a series of five, then a series of six. A trademark reminiscent, says Dr."J" of the megalithic work of pre-Inca civilizations.

"That is definitely not a road," Dr. "J" stated, back at the boat.

"Okay. Then what could it be?"

"My personal feeling," he said, "is that the whole fantastic complex represents the intelligent utilization, by ancient man, of materials appropriate for some ceremonial center. Remember that ancient sacred sites such as the geometric designs in prehistoric England, Stonehenge, or the Nazca plain in Peru, and megalithic work the world over involving pyramids, dolmens —

large, flat stones laid across upright stone pillars — etc., have virtually no point of reference with our own form of cultural evolution."

"Uhm, yeah," I said. I tried to get it, but it was a pretty far out concept for a Caibbean boat captain to chew on. I sometimes have a problem with history, even as far back as last month. Was this a "Simple boat captain moment?"

"Those civilizations were lost, swallowed by eons of time," he went on, lecturing as in his class – I am afraid, about ten eons over my head – "and by cataclysmic forces of a still-growing earth. The Pleistocene age was most recent, with the soaring Andes mountains pushed up only 30,000 years ago; Atlantis sinking into the ocean 11,500 years past.

"What is left of anything, after 10,000 years, is in the remains of time-worn rock. How giant stones could be moved in the remote past remains a mystery, but in one cave, a 20-ton stalagmite was removed from the ceiling, and balanced across the tip of a stalagmite, then fused there."

"Such majestic artifacts as these," he continued, "also the Bimini formation, are incomprehensible to us, unless, of course, we have the audacity to consider extraterrestrial intervention, or metaphysically generated energies." He spread his long, angular hands. "You see?"

"Uhm, I guess," I said. My mind was completely boggled.

The shifting sands of the Bahamas can cover tremendous areas of artifacts in very short time, Dr. "J" told me, but there are other areas where structures are still visible from the air. Things I did not have the capability to see. Ghost patterns, a creation of algae plants. Yes. But they were not real ghosts, just images.

Wherever the stones or walls are above the level of the bottom, algae attach and the patterns become highly visible, darker than the surroundings. That was how a "real estate development" showed up in a series of photographs, taken along the Old Bahama Channel. There was no known record of any modern city, or land mass. It appeared that a whole city was laid out on the shallow flats, with plots of land, an entire real estate scheme. There are still more puzzling conformations.

Around the island of Bimini, where Dr. "J" did a lot of research, he found a surprising underwater pattern which appeared to be made of cell structures, dark parallel lines forming hexagons and other geometric figures. It was about 1,000 feet long and resembled a giant footprint, with toes.

When he dove that area, Dr. "J" analyzed the pattern of hexagons, outlined by straight, dark rules as uniform as lines on a tennis court. They averaged 12 feet across, and at some points were depressed as though something below the surface caused the pattern to sink. The design was laid out with such mathematical precision, it seemed certain some architectural structure lay below.

In other areas of the Great Bahama Bank, perfectly straight lines stretch for miles, passing over and through all the irregularities of the bottom contours, as though scratched into the sand by some object suspended over the bottom. Even deep boat keels could not cause this phenomenon, Dr. "J" said, because the paths were uniform in width, two to four feet, but the water varied in depth. No marine plants grow in the grooves.

While the Bimini find was the beginning of his underwater discoveries, Dr. "J" said there was evidence of pre-cataclysmic civilizations that occupied this space long before that.

"What we found in the Yucatan was also pre-cataclysmic. The Loltun Cave was the focus of a tremendously ancient civilization. It was a huge cave, and at one point in some of its vestibule rooms, the ceilings rose to a hundred feet. There are goodness knows how many unexplored passages. I am certain there are deeper levels," he continued.

"But in these great, vaulted rooms are examples of pre-cataclysmic sculpture which are like the Masma sculpture of the Andes. In other words, it was part of the mountain, part of the geology. The ancient people carved on the great stalagmites. They got up on the ceiling – god knows how – and carved them. It is deep in the cave. I am sure even deeper passageways have been sealed up."

At another place, the north end of Bimini, is an area of water, three to five fathoms deep and crisscrossed by an intricate pattern , a gridwork of straight and curved lines. At one place, the lines emerge from the water and proceed across dry land. Even where they cross land, no vegetation grows.

Dr. Jones explained why nothing will grow there, and lost me temporarily. My head was beginning to fill up and couldn't expand into more heavy or outlandish ideas. I'm used to believing what I can hold in my hand.

Geologic time travels much farther than anything I might even guess.

"The lines where nothing grows were irradiated, by spacecraft," he maintained. "I was over the Nazca lines — those huge drawings of animals on the floor of the desert in Peru – and if you look at these figures from high in an airplane – the only way you can actually see them whole– they are a different color from their sur- roundings.

"Modern man didn't create them. In all these cases; the very antique carvings in England, the megalithic draw- ings on the chalk cliffs, and the lines underwater in the Bahamas … nothing grows in the immediate surround- ing area. I believe they were reserved as some sort of ceremonial sites."

I was a believer to this point, but the complexity soon got tougher for me to absorb.

"It is all related to space," Dr."J" expounded. "If you take an airplane and fly over the Tor – a huge hill at Dartmoor, England – you make out a huge Zodiac, 30 miles in circumference, with all of the 12 Zodiac sym- bols represented. Astrological concepts are also from space."

I admitted, "As a good Scorpio, I am into astrol- ogy, but outer space?"

Exactly when, and who the spacemen were, Dr. "J" was not positive, but cited instances of links with world- wide ancient civilizations, some that are difficult to ex- plain.

"The original spacemen probably come from Sirius, the Dog Star. There is still one African tribe which knows the Dog Star is a binary star, even though they do not know the significance of that.

"There is much that links the continents: the pyramids, used in religious rites, are common in Mexico and Egypt; the sacred shells used in rites; the idea of the trinity. The Celtic religion used a triangular shell with three spirals. It was also used in Ireland, Crete, Mexico, and the Mississippi Valley. In India, the God Shiva holds one in one hand.

"The sacred languages of the Kahunas in the Pacific and the Berbers in Africa are almost identical. Does that indicate a worldwide culture, or not?"

I was dumbfounded by this. Almost a foreign language to me. But I was fascinated, like watching a movie Orson Welles may have dreamed up, a "War of the Worlds," make believe, but not real. Sure I want to believe it, just like you. *That's Hollywood!*

"Okay," I murmured, "but what about that underwater pyramid, here?"

"We have sonar tracings of the pyramid. We know exactly where it is, and as soon as the weather is better we are going to dive and explore it. The base of the pyramid is 540 feet wide, and rises 420 feet high, similar in size to the Great Pyramid of Egypt, at 480 feet. It is a vital link in my study of the origins of life."

"You are writing that book? How does it go?"

"I try to pull all these thoughts together, on evolution and adaptation of zoogeography – the study of the distribution of animals – trying to correlate that with ancient continental masses."

"That will be one helluva book, I think. What do

your colleagues think about that? Are they impressed?"

"They won't even speak to me."

"Then they can't be very smart. In fact, total morons, I think."

"When we came back from Mexico," he said, "after discovering those very important artifacts, pre-cataclysmic finds, the archaeologists were all riled up. Buzzing like bees. They said I shouldn't have gone into the cave. They don't want to be disturbed. Like the priests who dared question the church, it's an inquisition.

"My study – this is just theory – is on a higher intellectual plane. A lot of PhDs have their notions, but it is now harder to deviate from the norm, into a new mode of thought. Ideas that won't fit prescribed theories abound in the scientific community, collectively known as 'erratics.' When an erratic comes along, they prefer simply to ignore it."

"But," I offered. "Your book, your study, would make changes in the way people look at the past, and maybe influnce the world future."

"Yes," he smiled, "It would foment a complete revolution in all thinking. It will reform every theory of religion, philosophy, paleontology. It will revise everything we have come to believe about the origins and evolution of man and the entire world."

"I can hardly wait." We hauled anchor and headed back to … reality? Whatever?

I think about Dr. "J" and his theories. Not a lot, because I too wonder how I might reform my evolution to fit better into the world, rather than working all day then looking forward to an occasional rum-soaked re-treat to Staniel Cay, or far Antigua, even lovely St. Lucia and environs. Whether our meeting was pre-destined I still have no idea, but if I was any benefit to that fine, singular person, I am greatly thankful.

Whether he was right about his theories, or not, one thing I am certain of. Someone, very long ago, did know how to pick up those giant stones, and build mag-nificent cities, to see the Earth from somewhere up in the sky, and make those rock/sand paintings you can only view from an amazing 1,000 feet overhead.

Dr. "J" passed on some years later, and appar-ently noone picked up his gauntlet to discover the whole story. I won't try to figure it out. I wish I could.

I'll have to leave that challenge to the next bright, brave, bold and adventurous scientist. Someone just like

My mentor, the *Genuine Indiana Jones*.

#

CAPT. CHUCK GNAEGY

Thirteen

Pirates in Caribbean History

Calico Jack Rackham was one of the few, but not the only Pirate who had females as crew. His knickname was about colorful raiment, instead of the rag-tag most Pirates wore. Jack's first command came when the Captain of an English warship, Neptune, refused to engage a French frigate. His crew mutinied, elected Rackham as Captain; then they pursued and sank the frigate. At New Providence awaiting orders, he saw a woman – Anne Bonny – and fell immediately in love, even though she was married to a sailor. Because of their affair, the Governor threatened to have Anne lashed for adultry. They stole a ship and dressed Anne as a man so the crew wouldn't rebel. A war ship was sent to capture them. Rackham and his crew were then tried in Jamaica; most hanged within a day. Anne Bonny and Mary Read were shipped to prison in London; both escaped the gallows by claiming to be pregnant. Calico Jack was eventually hanged, along with most of his crew.

Panama Lite: Pearls
From the Master

Don't Need a Cannon to be a Giant Killer

"You actually catch *hundred pound fish*," I said, not really believing, "on a *ten pound- test line?* A ten to one ratio. Why don't they break off?" The surprises were yet to come, and to be many.

"There are people who spend their lives fishing," said my friend Stan, "but they'll never see, or catch, as many different kinds of fish as we will in one day. That's not to mention 100-pound fish on 10-pound test line."

Easy for him to say. Not easy for me to climb his mountain. Fish somehow know it's me. My reputation always slips out ahead. For fish, it's ESP; they know I am an easy bully victim, and they're not about to slurp my worm. Any other goodie or fly I flash at them just lays there.

But this Stan, a master angler, has proven he knows how to find his target. A gen-u-wine, true life world multi-record holder, he horses in hundred+ pound tarpon on flimsy sticks, including a 12-lb. tippet that has stood for years. With a fly rod. Oh my. How could that be possible? If so, let me hear those pearls of wisdom.

We were on the paradisiacal Pacific Coast off Coiba, a tiny, palm-draped, wind-swept tiny paradise isle just off Panama / Costa Rica. My 44' trawler and I spent the season, before we embarked on a cruise through the Panama Canal and back into the Caribbean for summer.

Fishing is not, as a rule, my cup of tea. I am a sailor, a yachtie, a dabbler in many sea-things. Sure, I catch fish, sometimes, when I want dinner, or trolling behind a sailboat in the Gulfstream, or dropping a line over the side in a deserted, quiet anchorage anywhere in the islands.

However, to go out all day and catch a zillion fish for *sport,* then let 'em go? If that is *sport fishing* I can not grasp it. But would it be different if I were with a bona fide expert? Maybe he would slip me a few simple little secrets. Genuine pearls of wisdom, for king mackerel, queen blue marlin, non-canned gigantic tuna, sail, and waaa-hooo!

Stan rushed me down to the skiff right after breakfast, barely dawn. My pancakes were not even settled. We headed for Rancheria, a little sprit where big, craggy rocks vault up 100 feet from 40 fathoms out of the bluest ultamarine *agua* you'd ever see. A cathedral in the open sea. I could pretend I was Quasimodo, the hunchback of Notre Dame; he'd love to scuttle around this place of worship. Spume and foam bursting all around. Whoever was up in that sky was happy with the paintbrush on that particular day. Thank you, Jupiter, Pluto, or Venus, perhaps, making us all happy.

Stan unlimbered his spinning outfit. "I'll try a rainbow runner on 6-lb. line," he said. He rigged a tougher spool for me, with 15-lb. line on an ugly rod that had a sinister look. I was sure it didn't not like me.

"Morning is good for wahoo here," he said, smiling, "so is afternoon and evening." Yep. Seconds after our casts, a split second, pandemonium. "Hey, it's a double hook-up!"

"Wa-hoooo," he yelled. Grinned at me and dashed for the bow, reeling furiously. The guide swerved the center console boat crazily to chase his fish. It zoomed away at 90 mph and peeled off a couple hundred yards of line in a sec.

I lurched toward the bow – these little boats in calm seas bounce and chop like my trawler in a very nasty storm. There was a fish out there with my paw print on it. I jerked back on the rod to set the hook; my reel screamed and line stripped off in a blur. "Whee," I hollered. "It's headed for the South Pole."

Stan, his own rod bobbing, got excited about mine. "Look at that sucker go!" he said. He couldn't resist teaching me how he does this, thank goodness. "Now, when it runs in a long spurt like that, pinch the line in your fingers, to slow it down." A pearl? Perhaps.

I tried that, got third degree zig-zag burns on my thumb and forefinger. Marks might stay with the me forever. This fish needed air brakes, not a finger wave. It was a Donzi racing to Australia. "Hey, fish, didn't you feel that hook? It's in there." It was hauling gass.

Finally, worried my line would run right off the spool, I reached down to crank up the drag. Slower is better in this, I surmised, like a lot of other nice things. The line stretched, whined, popped. I muttered an unprintable.

Stan looked my way, annoyed. He held up his spinning rod. "Look, I am using six pound test line. Drag's loose, but I slow the fish down with my fingers against the spool."

His line zinged out, and after the initial surge he really clamped down until the fish stopped. He raised his arms high to pump it up, perhaps 400 feet out.

"The fish that jump or run a lot," he counseled, "are easier to fight, because they use up a lot more energy."

No sooner said than done, the fish burst toward the surface, didn't jump, spun in a big arc across the bow, left a foot wide foam track for 50 yards. It was not amused by some sharp piece of man made steel jammed in its beak. Then zoomed back down into the blue water. I saw, with my polarized sun glasses, the electric silver-blue torpedo whipping like a shoe-shine rag, zapping its head back and forth against the pull.

Stan pumped the rod high to gain a big bite of line, reeled down fast in a smooth motion. Fishy grudgingly yielded, circled to the top. The guide scooped it up in a jumbo-sized, two-handed net. Beauty. Big wahoo. Fight took 21 minutes.

"Hey, wait a minute," Stan said. "Jackpot, I think. "This is a big wahoo for 6-lb. spin. Maybe a record." He looked at the guide. "What do you think, Rito? Pesca grande?"

The guide shrugged, grinned. "Quince, veinte, quisas." A 15 to 20 pound fish here, off Coiba, was not enough to make him think of something else besides his big whole onion I saw him snacking on, like an apple. I guessed if you live here, you learn to like what they grow. (That was no *pearl* onion).

Stan extracted a hand scale and a record list right there, from his tackle box. That guy, I thought, if he shot a bear, or dinosaur, he'd have the stuff to mount it in his tackle box. Checked the ISFA list. A record. Confirmed. We hauled butt back to the marina to grab a photo and make it official, logged it in before it lost water and shrunk. Every little ounce, to a sportfisher, is its own reason for living.

That was the ninth record wahoo for this area, including ISFA 4, 6, 8 lb.test, IGFA 6, 12, and SWFRA 6, 10, 12, 15 lb. tippets. They date back as far as 20 years ago when Bob Montgomery ran his once fabled Club Pacifico, now no longer in business.

It was all new to me. I expect a fish to be good to eat, so I get the charcoal ready. This record hoorah was fun, if it turned you on. The Fishing Club trumpeted a long list of records: Pacific barracuda, Spanish mackerel, Black marlin, Cubera snapper, in all weight and line sizes.

"All that time," I said, "I thought you were drowning a rainbow runner."

"That wahoo thought so, too," he fired back.

"Eighteen and a half pounds," I said, "on 6 lb. test,

not bad. Three to one ratio." That's how the masters rate their catch. But ten to one is the 'awesome' category, the big kahuna they want. Like that hundred pound fish on 10 lb. line. Any better than that is *Nirvana*.

"Not bad. But not a giant."

"Tomorrow, we'll try another hot spot, and the next day, we'll go for sailfish," he said. "You'll eat your words."

"One thing I didn't tell you," I ventured.

"What was that?"

"Day after tomorrow is my birthday. Will I get a giant sail to decorate my cake?"

"Count on it."

A thing that stands out, fishing with an expert, is his meticulous attention and preparation of equipment and gear. We spent the whole evening tying leaders for next day, rigging double lines, measuring exact lengths to be sure the rules are met, no mishaps. Perfect. He showed me how. Blood knots, Bimini Twist knots, fly line with a trace length of 12 inches including the double line, the knot, and the coffee stained wire leader. Hooks, which seemed so sharp in those little plastic boxes; we honed each hook with a pocket sharpening stone, triangulating to scalpel sharp, so when you drag it across your thumbnail it digs right in. Now it becomes lethal.

Rods and reels are double checked, screw for screw, bolt for bolt, guide for guide; swivels tested, and lines – plainly marked by the maker as 10-lb. test – but individually tested by us to be sure they are well under the minimum. So when used, a 10-lb. test is closer to 8 pounds breaking strength. Even a fraction over 10 lbs.

goes into the 12-lb. class.

At dawn we bolted down a bowl of cereal and a plum, coffee, rushed out to the boat, a 24-foot catamaran center console fisherman. "Hey," I said, "why are we running? Don't we have all day?"

Guide Rito waited for us, munching on a giant clove of garlic, his breakfast. A nice guy, but I hoped he didn't breathe on me. He didn't speak much English; and we had barely a little espanol. But he understood "Sailfish." (Pez vela).

In 20 fathoms of water just off the mainland there is plenty of nutrient to bring in smaller fish, which lure in the big 'uns. IGFA 12-lb. record for wahoo - 74 pounds.

"The wahoo is so quick, we'll have to troll fast to interest them," Stan said. "Bedsides, they have such light-sensitive eyes, they go deep when the sun is bright. They like cloudy days." The guy was a walking encyclopedia on fish. I should have asked him what they'd do if their ol' lady ran around on them when they are away on a fishing trip. Uhm, do fish *phish*?

Not quick enough on that. In a second Stan was hooked up with a wahoo that grabbed his jig, but instead of running, flashed right straight at us, zoomed past the boat just under the surface.

"Look at that acceleration," Stan marvelled. Look at him screech away, burning rubber from a standing start. No other fish is as fast as this drag racer."

It barreled in a right angle turn from the bow. Suddenly the line went slack. Off.

Rito spat a wad of garlic into the sea.

"Aguja…hound-fish. He see line go past, drag bubble. He think something to eat. He snap it. Aguja is needle-fish grown up."

I dropped my white feathered jig about 40 yards astern. Strike – right away – before I took a breath. Whipped line off , then reversed field, charged the boat, criss-crossed back and forth, dove deep and shook its head no,no,no.no. Arched back, I gained a few feet of line, reeled down quick. In a second it was in the boat, gaffed, a nice 27 pounds.

By the time that afternoon was over, I hooked a dozen more and landed seven, all 20 to 30 pounds. I allowed as how a 30 pound fish is no runt of the litter. Stan smiled, "We're catching these 'smaller' fish because our lines are so light we csn't use heavy jigs. When we troll fast enough for wahoo, the jigs come up higher, and that's where the smaller fish are. If we used heavier jigs they'd go deeper, where the bigger fish are."

Then in quick succession we landed a yellow-fin tuna, a nice bonito, couple of jack, and a beautiful mahi (green dolphin) that escaped when a tiny black swivel broke. It was okay last night, I checked it myself.

Next day we headed for 'frijoles,' a small pile of rocks nicknamed 'the beans,' lying just outside a deep channel. Good place for big wahoo, tuna, amberjack, any other big game fish you can name.

That bright morning we were into Allison tuna. In little time we released two good tuna, and an amberjack which stubbornly turned its body sideways for almost half an hour before it said uncle, and a wahoo I thought was the grandaddy of all, but turned out to be foul-hooked in the side, and weighed 'only' 30 pounds. Was I getting the hang of this?

Another pair of twins threw themselves at our jigs, and I was beginning to think nothing of a double or triple odds on my 15 lb. line. On the next strike I dashed for the bow as this fish led us 300 yards going away. I pinned the line to my cork handle as instructed. It was a bigger fish, stronger than I had on before.

It hung in there, giving no quarter, then suddenly eased. I reeled as fast as I could. No nice guy this. Stubborn, unmovable. Sat tight, like it was waiting for the sun to go down. Sulked for hours down there, while I grunted and sweat..

"Pressure it," Stan urged. "Tighten up your drag a little. Pump!"

The rod was bent almost doubled and would not yield. I was honking on it. Started moving away, then it ripped off a quick hundred feet more. My arms were creaking. Stan was taunting me like a linebacker on a quarterback. Sweat was streaming down my arms and neck. I felt like the little kid who wants to go pee.

"Hell," Stan yelled in my ear, "you're letting it rest. That fish is down there eating a leisurely lunch. Hell, It doesn't even know it's caught!"

I thought it was a really big wahoo. Hoped. Sixty to eighty pound fish come through there, they migrate and breed in that area. The fish zipped around at first, then got stubborn and decided it didn't want whatever I wanted to give it, which was a big gaff in the back of its neck. Agitated, I wanted that fish.

Finally, after a grueling hour and twenty minutes, I

managed to pump it up out of the depths. The brown, sinister shape edged toward the stern. It was not my prize wahoo.

"Tiburon," Rito muttered. "Shark."

My hook glistened between the rows of triangular teeth, wedged in so it couldn't chomp the wire leader. Banged its head angrily against the transom.

A brown shark about nine feet long, 150 pounds. On 15-lb. line that was a worthy catch – ten to one. Arms aching, I dragged it slowly alongside. That was a hefty, toothy, dangerous animal. We didn't want it aboard, or even to chance a gaff . Rito dispatched it with a diver's bang-stick – a 12-gauge shotgun shell on a spear. Bye-bye shark.

Hundred-fifty pounds. Ten to one. So, I was now a giant-killer third class, on my first real fishing expedition. Thank's to Stan's well regulated instructions. If I had been alone, I wouldn't have put a three inch porgy into the fish well.

But I knew there were plenty of good catches off Coiba. Giant marlin. Last year, I learned, even though casting for snapper from the beach, a surprised angler hooked into a huge, cruising black marlin, which leapt out of the surf and grabbed his darter. For a few seconds he gloried on an unlimited world record. He was a minnow tackling a whale. In a few more seconds, of course, the fish whisked away without even a thank-you, taking the souvenir plug, half his line, plus his pending world record with it.

One party fishing for black marlin off Coiba hooked 11 of those blue rockets in a span of 2 1/2 hours.

Meanwhile, back at the skiff, after a hard strike off the Frijoles, Stan had a hook-up for 15 minutes before the fish got off. Threw the hook. As he reeled in, the shiny hook broke water, straight as a pencil, waved like soldering wire. What sort of fish could straighten a 5/0 hook and not break 12 lb. spinning line? Try to unbend one of those with your fingers. Never do it. Maybe a big shark just clamped it in its teeth.

They are out there, too. A big wahoo was spurting around so fast it left a wake clear around the boat. Stan had it on. "Something's after it," he said. "When a fish moves like that – scared — a big shark or cubera snapper is chasing it. Look, something hit it just then." He pointed aft of the stern. "Look at that. Damn!"

For half a millisecond I saw the gory snapshot of the wahoo, big one, maybe 60 lbs., disappearing like a marshmallow into the maw of a huge white-tip shark. As it rolled, belly up, no blood, just one gulp. We stared in awe. The 12 foot-long body rolled over and smacked its jaws, flashed a big grin, dove to the equator.

"You ready to take some underwater photos now?" Stan said.

"I think I forgot my fins." I mumbled. " I better wait for another day."

Next day we were off for the sail grounds at Punta Clara, a short run through 4-foot seas. We saw, in the distance, mounds of other islands popping out of the Pacific, emerald periods and exclamation points of the Seirra Madre chain, poked up as beauty marks on the wide, wild blue. Gorgeous. That is a decoration job that must have been done by an expert. Thank you, Zeus.

Stan gestured off the starboard bow. "Watch those frigate birds. They see the fish from up there, and they follow a big marlin or sail into a school of bait. If it comes in range, they dive down and get one before Mr. Marlin does."

Now the sky was darkening into rain, we saw the streaks across the sky. Gonna get wet. Who gives a damn when sailfish fish are out there, stalking our baits, lunging at our clever feathers?

Our two orange squid teasers skipped lightly in our wake, and Stan uncoiled a pile of loops from his fly rod. He wanted a big Pacific sail on fly, with a whippy nine-foot fly rod.

The drill: I'd handle the teaser — when a big sail came behind to grab it, I'd let him take the squid, mouth it, then jerk it away, teasing. After two or three tries, Mr. Sail would eat a handful of cockleburrs. Then Stan would swoosh the real fly right ahead of it.

"Mira!" Rito shouted. "Pez vela!" "Sailfish!"

Off to one side the big sail arrowed up and slashed into a foaming geyser. We swung wide to slap the teaser right across its nose; its black stiletto carved a Zorro. Zzzip!

Slash! Swoosh! Gulp!

The sail snatched the squid teaser in one grab. I waited two seconds, then jerked it away, right out of the sword-mouth. Did it twice more. The sail lit up in a jillion colors, green, blue, gold, white. Pulsing like Las Vegas neon, enraged. Magnificent. Then Stan plopped the white popper bug in front of its maw. Strike!

On for only a couple of seconds, then off. It charged right up to the transom, hunting for the popper. That fish was mad as hell. Or hungry enough to eat a boat.

Stan swished it out again. Took again, spit it out again. Gave up. Took off, pouting. Ten minutes, two more sails. Stan said, "We'll use both sticks now."

I brought out my 15-lb. casting set-up, with a translucent squid on a 5/0 hook. If the first wahoo was a baptism of fire, and the ten to one shark genuine paydirt, then this would be the entire honking Magilla.

"Rito, handle the teaser," Stan coached. "The fish will come up slashing. You keep your rod high. When you see the bill stuck straight up behind the lure, the fish has its mouth wide open. You drop your rod tip and the bait goes down its throat. Drop back, let the fish swallow it. Strike it four or five times. A sail has a bony mouth."

It happened just like he wrote the script.

I got it right. "Iiii Goooooottttt Iiiit!" I yelled. Line shrieked off my reel. Rain started pounding down then but I didn't feel a thing except that freight train tearing off my line. Braced my knees at the gunnels. Back into it. Rito gunned the engine after the wild one and I reeled madly. The line begain to stretch. "Coming up!" Stan yelled.

"When it jumps, drop your rod, give it slack so it doesn't shake the lure."

The big sail speared up and tail walked 30 yards before it crashed back. I bowed to it like he said. Then it was up again. And again. "Yee-ow!? I screamed. "You see that? Silver and gold and neon blue bars? Electric! The slot machine vomiting a million bucks!"

Stan was right behind me. "Hold that line against the cork handle. After it runs awhile you tighten drag one turn only, but don't break it off."

I was not about to lose that one if I could help it. *Sport Fish?* Now I saw what *sport fishing* really is. That torpedo jumped twelve, fifteen times, an Aegena rocket. My arms turned to lead. Pumped it back again.

He coached, "If the fish jumps many times then dives, it can't stay down long because its air bladder fills up at the surface."

More jumps, the fish had a trampoline in its tail bone. Then suddenly it was alongside the boat, fight gone. Waved its bill like D'Artagnon. "How long did that last?" I whimpered, bushed. "Thirty-five minutes," Stan said.

Rito grabbed the leader and Stan grabbed the bill in both hands, thumbs facing each other so if the fish lunged, it couldn't stab him in the gut. Hauled it in.

We did not gaff this broad-shouldered fish. Stan did a quick tape measure, length and girth, estimated its weight at 110 lbs. – no record at stake, but a very nice sail – a beautiful sail, and I did not want to kill such a gorgeous playmate-foe. Was that soft-soap, or what? Awww, Cap'n Chuuuck…

I kept it on the wall in my head, a mind snapshot. I wanted it to live a good life in the ocean, if that is what it wanted. The fish on deck, exhausted, blue and gold stripes fading to gray. Giving up. I didn't want it to die because of me. Strange hunter to deny the trophy. It was only trying for a snack and made a minor, as they say, error in judgement.

We hurried to snap a few photos, then pumped the tired fish up and down in the water by the tail until it showed a flicker of life. Waggled its tail. With a last shove, it swam away, wobbly, but alive to eat another squid, another day. That gladiator leapt for me 18 times. Thank you, my first sailfish.

In the next couple of hours we raised a dozen more sails, then headed for "wahoo rocks." It was barely lunch-time. Time goes so fast when you're having ...fish.

We ended the day with 14 fantastic lords-a-leap-ing Pacific sailfish raised and one (er, masterfully) landed, 18 wahoo hooked and a dozen in the fish box, with new world records to register, and half a dozen other species taken and released. So, this was *Sport Fishing*?

I would depart next day back to the Caribbean, with a giant tackle box full of memory pearls, and perhaps a couple of fish tales, maybe a few elementary how-tos I did not have before. I would also have a great deal more respect for the guys and gals who spend a large part of their lives -- and invest gobs of money -- pursuing this great sport. I would take with me a reason for my harbored, new, secret infatuation for *Sport Fishing*.

That night, after we punched down a fine dinner at the lodge, suddenly the lights went out, and before we could ask what happend, in marched the chef at the head of a parade with all his cooks and cohorts, bearing a round, fat, candle-loaded birthday cake. All singing.

To Capt. Chuck . How could they know?

"You spilled the beans," I accused. I was embarrassed, flushing.

"Oh Yeah," Stan stuck out his hand. "I meant to wish you, Happy Sailfish!"

#

Capt. Chuck Gnaegy

Fourteen

Pirates in Caribbean History

Sir Francis Drake, the "Gentleman Pirate," held many distinctions: Vice Admiral of the Fleet against the Spanish Armada; First Englishman to circumnavigate the globe in his "Golden Hind"; Royalty lineage for four generations; Commander of his first ship at age 20; Knighted by Elizabeth I., Drake conquered the Spanish Silver Train at Nombre de Dios, 1573, doing his duty for England, for a fortune in gold. In 1579 he established "New England" a port north of San Francisco Bay. He is revered in the Virgin Islands; in St. Thomas there is "Drake's Seat" high up on the mountain where it is said he monitored Spanish Galleons sailing the straits below, waiting for a chance to pounce. He captured the city of St. Augustine (Florida) as well as Cartagena and Santo Domingo in the Caribbean. Though considered a hero in England, Spain still regards him as bloodthirsty Pirate.

Sail Away to Paradise
Part 1

Escape the Grind, to Your Own Kingdom

"Argh! Argh, Argh," Richard had croaked in his Blackbeard froggy voice. "Big boomers. Those don't ever blow this far south. Relax." He nodded. Jerked his head back. "Hey, hand me that rum."

Yet it was boiling blackness out there. Stretched horizon to horizon. Left to right, streaked with strange, searing blackness and alabaster white with carmine red fingers. I could smell the danger, the lightning, almost touch the ragged edges dragging spikey tails across lumpy seas; feel the raw wind scald my skin and tear at the clattering sails. But when it happened it was a lightning strike.

Three seconds. 'Heavy wind' was more like hallucination. Close-hauled, the first gust smacked us sideways, flapped us down like a 300-lb. defensive tackle who wants to eat what he kills. Too frigging late' was also not strong enough. All hell broke wild and loose.

Dangling in green water up to my armpits, my legs

thrashed in foaming nothingness or whatever was down there. The sailboat's deck was half under also, up to its hip-pad pudendum, careened onto its beam ends. Green sea water gushed into the cockpit, plunging down the cabin hatchway.

This was no Optimist pram; a 35-foot full keel small cruising 'yacht,' loaded with everything for a comfortable liveaboard lifestyle. But in those seconds and what followed, we were about to find out about living – or buying it — on the bottom, wherever that was.

Richard grunted "Arghhh, arghh, aaarrgghhh!" He invariably had dry heaves in any wild encounter with the weather, or the ocean. Wrestling the tiller, trying to veer upwind, he snorted, "Drop that main!"

I hardly heard him in the roaring gale, the bedlam. But I knew what he wanted, what had to be done. I jumped onto the deckhouse roof. He fumbled with the main sheet, ripped it off the cleat. The boom zipped out, the ship veered and almost righted itself. The boom shot all the way out, perpendicular to the boat, and in a split second I was clinging to it with all my strength. Feet and legs in the foaming sea, blubbering a prayer to Mars and Saturn to get off my sorry asp and let me get this boat stopped from its suicide into the depths. Screaming wind was a force that would not be conquered. Its noise was a locomotive rolling over us, tearing at our skin, eyes, mouths. One small split and it plunged for invasion, swinging for the knockout.

The belly of the mains'l was in the water, edges heaped on top of me like Ahab's white whale. The boat careened, zapped its side all the way into the drink. Wind spilled away and we instantly rebounded, almost upright. I struggled to unwind the halyard off the cleat and tear the line loose. Most of the main had crashed down on me, covered the whole boat. Now it was gyrating over again in the wave pattern, trying to deep six itself, the sail, and me in the foaming sea. I was coughing, spurting up salt geysers. Gagging, gasping for a clean breath.

She groaned and lurched almost upright again. Crash! The sail thrashed down, totally. Slammed down on the deck. The heavy keel flipped us quickly upright. Like a rag doll, I was tossed back onto the cabin roof, smothered in wet sail, tangled in a rope halyard noose. Surrounded by lumping eight foot seas that aggressively gnawed at our port beam for lunch. Trying to put us under, asunder.

Richard fired the engine and it roared, revving up too high. He threw it in gear to gain quick momentum. Then in a split second I heard a splat, a twang, a weird thump; the engine ground down, stalled out. Quit. Richard's main sheet, thrown out, had zapped under the boat and wrapped the propeller. Wind shrieking, blasting spume all over us. Waves trying to mount us like a dog pack in heat off those eight foot seas.

Suddenly I was sure we were really up the creek without an oar, nor a north star to steer her by. Bye!

How in the name of Richard-Monte-Carlo-Argh!-Argh!-Moore did I get myself into this mess?

It had started off sweet and slow. We were in my favorite place — *One thousand miles from reality* — I call it, sailing comfortably, light breeze off the starboard bow, just out of Georgetown, Exuma, away down in the bottom bowels of the Bahama chain, set to cross into the Carib. But all was not strawberries and Cool Whip just yet. If yesterday's northern sky was any prophet, we'd never get there in one piece anyway. I had felt it creeping up on us, but warnings to the Captain were disregarded, poo-poohed. He knew what he wanted, and the sky was obligated to deliver. That kind of guy.

Our course would be straight east towards funky Calabash Bay, then around Long Island and east then southward to Rum Cay, Land Rail Point. The end of the Bahamas, Mayaguana, Great Inagua Cay, and overnight across to the Dominican Republic. Puerto Plata, Samana, the raw Eden country that God put there then seemed to forget.

Our course, strangely enough, would put us on the track of Columbus' original sail. After he "discovered" "San Salvador," – Grand Turk – he sailed south toward "Santa Maria de Concepcion" – Rum Cay, "Fernandina" – Long Island, and "Isabela" – Crooked Island; our intended route exactly.

"Those clouds," I told him, "that is a virile, dangerous frontal system. Yesterday the front shut down the Miami airport for three hours when I tried to leave." I flew down just for this trip.

That was when he pulled his Pirate's bandana down to his eyebrows and cranked a smirk out of his bearded mug. "Those fronts," He growled, "Avast, me hearty, they never come this far south. We are in the Carry-bee-hind Sea, for godsake. That is nothing but a herd of little baby lambs. Aarrgh! Aarghh!"

He said that a lot, "Aargghh." His way to emphasize anything he was saying that was not important enough to listen to anyway. He thought he was Captain Blood, or maybe Charlie Brown, scolding Lucy wotsher-name.

But I was watching warily at those clouds. Like a herd of buffalo along the entire north horizon now, growing, milling around, sniffing at each other, packing themselves together, maybe for a stampede. They were dark grey, moving fast. A long, long way off.

But where we were, in the soft winded Carib, there was light, bright sun and happy grins. It's what we all want. Never mind reality. Perhaps.

At five or six knots it would take half a day to sail over to Calabash Bay, where we'd anchor out overnight. Richard and I differed on time. I am a morning person. I wake up quick and fast, I want leave at six ayem; then we'd be there already. He likes to drink and carouse all night, get away about three in the afternoon, then party all night.

It's his boat. He is Captain of *MoonDancer*. This was a 35-foot Endurance, wooden, half rotted sailboat, sloop rigged, with tattered sails and a head that spreads its nostril piercing stench into a gory message, downwind like 3-Mile Island, or grandpa's outhouse that ought to have been torched on Halloween a dozen years ago.

I was only the crew. He brought me along because I put up with him and do what he says. He needed an able-bodied crew. Without a boat for the first time in years, I was looking for adventure.

We were friends, of a type. I was the more reserved

intellectual, tall, slender, educated, conservative one. He was the town drunk, short and bald-headed, an ego the size of Shaq O'Neil, paunchy, with a full black beard and a bandana tied around his bald head like the Count of Monte Cristo (he thought), raving all night with a bottle of rum down his hatch.

Even so, when he was awake and sober, we'd have some very entertaining discussions and plenty of lies to tell about our mutual love and respect for the sea, the islands we have seen, wild trips we've had, some of the same things we like, women, and people we love and hate. I think, and he thinks, we are good together, sparring partners. Maybe he had a part of me that's missing, and I had a part he would like. We tolerated, enjoyed each other, good buddies.

One other small inconsistency: all my life I've made my living by my wits; now as a yacht captain. He sold his *Consolidated Pest Control* business in Denver, Colorado, and retired to live on his boat in Key Largo.

People called us *"The Odd Couple."*

Richard cranked up the transistor radio to some island music, and brought out a pair of drumsticks, clacking out a rhythm, humming to the music, some reggae bongo beat from Jamaica. He loved Hairy Belly (Bellafonte). I was checking the sky again, and the radio, to see if anyone except me was monitoring that mass migratory bison formation. It had been a terrific storm at Miami, crippling the city for hours. Not easy to do. No one else down here cared.

But it was closer now. "Richard," I said, "this herd of buffalo-lambs is gaining on us. I can almost hear their thunder. Look over there. Those clouds are humping up one on top of the other. It is slipping over the sun. This is a front. A very fast, rapid, nasty front that is about to jump right on top of us. A line squall."

"Aarrgghh! I told you, relax. How about some lunch?"

"Okay." I went below to fix some sandwiches. I got involved in that, checked the charts, checked my ditty bag, and a little later brought up a platter of goodies. Some cold cuts, cheese, olives, carrots, bread, and beer. But I saw then, as I came up the three steps from the galley, that front was almost on top of us. The galloping herd, in full stampede, was thundering at our corral doorstep.

He was napping, perched over the tiller, asleep.

"Dick! For Chrissake. Look! Those buffalo are an entire Montana regiment now, covering up the sun. The wind is singing fresh. This is no drill! Those are goddam nasty clouds. A very black, ominous front!"

He jerked up momentarily, paled. "Squall line!" Suddenly awake. Pulled his head-gear down. "Arrgghh, I'll start the engine. Get that main down. Now!"

I slapped the tray down on the bench seat, and vaulted up for the cabin roof. I was almost to the main halyard when the first gust smacked us.

That first gust was a roller coaster drop that smashed us sideways. I grabbed onto the mast with one arm and stretched for the halyard with the other. Too frigging late.

Suddenly I was in the water up to my armpits, my feet thrashing in deep green sea, no bottom. The sail boat was careened onto its beam end; slobbering foam water was slam-dunking over the deck into the cockpit, racing down the cabin hatchway.

Richard was arghing, clawing at the tiller, trying to get us upright. "Drop that main!" he yelled. He grappled with one hand on the tiller and the other on the main sheet. Ripped the main sheet free. Now it was loose off the cleat and the boom rocketed all the way out, right angles to the boat. I was hugging onto the boom like a three year old who wanted his mommy, cursing, blubbering a prayer to whomever, I'm sorry for every sin I have committed on purpose or by accidental inclusion.

The mains'l latched on to me like swaddling clothes and I was helpless in its loving power. But when it splatted all the way into the drink, the wind spilled out, and we suddenly heaved almost upright. I was tossed like a frisbee back on deck. Eyes clenched, I unwrapped the halyard off the cleat and whipped off the line. Then I was suddenly enveloped in a mountain of dirty white, half the total of soggy orlon/canvas, gasping for breath and kicking my feet against whatever that was under me, the deck or cabin top. At least it was something. Then we gyrated over again, the boat was trying to deep six itself with half the sail, and me, over the side.

For a second it tried to right again, then the rest of the sail slammed all the way to the deck. The keel took over and we swung upright, shot like a see-saw. I was swooshed back onto the cabin roof, still submerged in wet sail, rope halyard wrapped around my waist, legs, and arms. The seas punched at us, like heavyweights

swinging haymakers. Slam. Bang. Blammo. We were surrounded by Geronimo's entire kayaking army, all toma-
hawking our port beam. They wanted to bury us with
General Custer and Joshua Slocum.

Richard fired the engine and it caught, revving up
too high. He threw it in gear to gain quick momentum.
That's when in a split second I heard the taut, weird
thump, with the engine grinding down, stalled out. Gave
up. The main sheet Richard had let run dove under the
stern and wrapped its skinny arm around the propeller.
Now we were really up Schlipt Creek without a canoe,
or a constellation to steeer by.

The squall was in full cry. Wind shrieking, blasting spume over us off eight foot waves. How quick it can
change. I whipped out my bowie knife and sawed off the
jammed sheet. No difference. The engine still blank, still
silent. Dead.

"Got to get us into the wind!" Dick yelled, horsing
the tiller all the way starboard. The wind momentum
dragged the stern around, sail still in the water, until we
were head on. I groped my way onto the cabin roof and
hauled the halyard. The main inched upward, then popped
as wind filled it. I ground on the winch until it was nearly
up, then cleated down the halyard. No way I could horse
it up tight, but it would give us some way now.

Dick used the other sheet to get us steady. The wind
was still screaming and driving us across the mounting
waves. That old boat had not danced this Virginia reel in
a very long time. She was complaining, bitching, but
moving her gross, rotten ass like a fat lady with a torch

up her gonzaga. Like never before.

I surveyed the boat forward. Dick had a dozen gas and diesel cans lashed to the stanchions for future use down island; and when the boat heeled so far, a couple of them started to spew fuel down the deck in long red runners. Most of it sloshed over the side, out the scuppers. But plenty was still with us. The air was foul with fuel smell.

Dick yelled at me over the wind song – song, hell, this was a Valkyrie chorus, those maidens who whisk the killed heroes off to Valhalla – led by the fattest, loudest divas in all creation, and they have got their eyes for us. "Hey," he yells, " Take the tiller. I got to go below!"

What can be below at a time like this? I took it in an instant. From there I could glance down inside the cabin. In the storm tossed interior, It was an incredible mess, everything that was stored in bookcases, drawers, lockers, oven, even the 300-horse 110-volt generator, all was heaped up in a gigantic pile in the center of the cabin. A mound three feet high.

And in the middle, on top the pile, perched Capitano Richard, Count of Monte Cristo. What? He was smoking a cigar!

The gas fumes were so thick you could slice and dice them into cubes, and he had plopped there and lit a butt! Why we were not half way to heaven by now from an explosion is beyond my weirdest imagination. But it did not blow.

I figured if it didn't already, it was not going to. I sank back onto the tiller seat and counted my blessings. How many of them could I have left? The sea still wild and crazy, but moaning now instead of the shriek, the boat was still pounding up and down on the roller coasters, spewing fuel spray and an oil slick downwind, but it was not yet destroyed. We were still alive, and afloat for the time being.

The wind shifted, suddenly clocked around to northwest, and so I knew the front had lurched past, but we were still pounded with heavy wind, and the boat was humping us, trying her best to wrestle the wind and seas. I shoved the tiller over to a port tack. We were going back, to lick our wounds and start over tomorrow, or whenever.

He did not want to go back. "We make Calabash Bay tonight. Aargh. We got all day tomorrow to free up the prop, sew up the rips in the sail, and get this stuff put away. We are going on. Sail on, oh ship of state!"

"Not likely," I retorted. "We are not sailing anywhere in this washtub until I am ready to go."

"You sound just like my wife. Argh. Arggh!"

"I am not your wife. But I am not going on. And you aren't, without me."

He stood there, Stunned. "Gimme the tiller."

"No."

"Get your hands off my tiller!"

"Like hell. You stand back there or I will deck you, little fat man, tie you up with adhesive tape, gag you, and stuff your sorry ass under that pile of shit in your living room!"

"ARRRGGGhhh! Argh, Argh, Argh!"

"I mean it, Dick. Back down," I said. You know I am a second degree black belt in Tae Kwan Do."

"Argh Argh. I am going below."

"Why?"

"To get the rum."

"Okay."

Ten seconds later he was on deck again. He was brandishing, not the rum, but a small semi-auto pistol, a .32 caliber German WWII aviator's side arm. Grimly, he said, "I am in command here. Now."

"We are still going back."

He stuck his arm up in the air and fired off two quick shots. They sounded puny. Pop-pop.

I kept my eyes steady on the course. Not moving. He brought the pistol up and fired two more. Pop. Pop. Something was wrong with the way they sounded. Flat, ineffective. I owned guns all my life. I am an avid target shooter, quail hunter, and I fired expert with every weapon they threw at me in Ranger training.

He did not move. Then I realized, suddenly, why they sounded funny. They are old ammo, hardly ever effective, or... of course.

"Hand me the pistol," I said. "And those blanks. We are going back."

He sat down on the cockpit bench. Deflated. Grinned, sickly.

"Argh Argh. How did you know that?"

"They are not the same. I have been there. Done that. I know the difference."

"Okay. I am getting the rum."

"One second." I reached over and snatched the gun from his hand. Tucked it in my pocket. Just in case. "Okay, we'll drink rum when we are safe in the harbor."

I learned one thing from Captain Richard that day I had never thought of before, a fine cruising tenet, besides the silly blank discovery.

"Always look back," he said as we left the last marker out of Georgetown. "You might have to come back in at night."

And that is exactly what we did. Night falling, we crept past the incoming marker, inside two narrow slots in the reef, to find a wide spot in the bay channel. By then it was black dark, and unsafe to proceed farther with our puny lights and the minimal navigational aids they have down there.

We dropped the anchor. Popped on the anchor light. Richard went below and emerged with two seal-unbroken bottles of Barbancourt Rare, Premium rum of the Dominican Republic. A sipping delight.

We broke the seals. Pulled the corks. Saluted each other. Down the hatch. We would drink them dry before we fell into a welcome, stuporous sleep.

"I would not really shoot you," he mumbled later, in apology.

"And I would not intentionally break both your arms and legs. Unless I had to."

"Arrrrgghh! Arrgh Arggh Arggh!"

#

PIRATES, PEARLS & PARADISE

Capt. Chuck Gnaegy

Fifteen

Pirates in Caribbean History

Jean LaFitte became famous in U.S. history books after he helped Andrew Jackson during the War of 1812 against the British. While LaFitte was a New Orleans shop owner, he saw Pirate prizes sailing from the New World, laden with jewels, gold, silver. A known womanizer, friend to high officials, he had a ship with guns and a Pirate crew, to prey on ships in the Gulf and Caribbean. So successful his fleet grew to a dozen vessels, the scourge of waters surrounding Florida, Cuba; the Caribbean to Honduras, Nicaragu, Haiti, Dominican Republic. From mines in Central and South America, Spain's Conquistadores loaded ships with stolen treasure, for Ferdinand and Isabella. When the Governor posted a reward of $750 for any ship to capture LaFitte; From his HQ at Barataria Bay, he brazenly offered twice that for the Governor's head. An outlaw, he still loved New Orleans. By 1814 the British attacked Jackson at New Orleans. LaFitte helped defeat them. He was pardoned, moved his Piracy HQ to Galveston, Texas. Then, forced to leave, he torched the town; and still continued Pirating off Central and South America.

Treasure Islands:
Dig Yourself a Fortune

Hurricane's Kiss: Pirate Gold Dubloons Emeralds, Diamonds; Out There

Black clouds. We moved along the beach at Padre Island; the telltale pings of our metal detectors pulsed loudly in unison, like cell phones gone crazy. Five yards apart, we knew – hoped – it meant something there was more important to us than the lightning and thunder boiling up the coast. We would stay as long as we dared; searching for lost cargo of sunken treasure galleons.

The thirst for sunken treasure, gold, pieces-of-eight, made it seem worth taking a chance, and after all, how many people actually are struck by lightning on the beach? We both dropped down on our knees and began digging at the sand with fingers and entrenching tools. The ping spot was half the size of a living room, a gift from the recent hurricane. She had thrown up enough bottom onto the wide beach that there could be anything under there. The 'anything' we hoped for, greedily dug for, was Jean LaFitte's legacy — gold and silver of Spain's treasure fleet the Pirate had buried, or lost at sea when his Pirate battlewagons sunk the treasure galleons, or themselves ran aground on the reefs and rocks.

When hurricane winds drove a treasure ship towards shore, it first had its bottom ripped out as it was rocketed against sunken boulders, by 120 mph winds and 20-to-40- foot seas, spewing its cargo for miles. With LaFitte's bandit ships after them; or the pirate ships themselves after plundering the galleons, fleeing weather, millions in jewels and treasure were strung along miles of shoreline at Padre Island, or Brazos Pass.

Few records from the Spanish Archives in Madrid actually tell of the locations; most crews and Captains didn't survive to give exact references. All that was recorded were dates and ports the ships left; with veiled references to what treasure was actually aboard. Those figures were only the official data, and failed to include private treasure horded by the Captains and crew, plus hidden, illegal shipments that went unrecorded, smuggled for the benefit of higher-ups in government.

The same was true on Florida's east coast off Sebastion Inlet, just south of Melbourne/Palm Bay, where hurricane winds scattered the Spanish Plate Fleet's treasures over beaches and offshore reef gardens.

Our quest was similar to another I knew about, where two treasure seekers had struggled against rising winds and waves in the same area. Within two hours they collected a cluster of 18 Pieces-of-Eight, gold dubloons. They wrapped the booty in a red bandana and feverishly dug for more. Two hours later they had pulled out old wine bottles, cannon balls, musket barrels, trappings of a sought-after sunken treasure ship, but no more of the avidly sought after gold,silver, and precious gems.

By then the wind was lashing them with stinging sand, while rain and an incoming tide rushed water into their digs. Frantic as the lightning storm boomed around them, they piled up a heap of rocks, a stele to mark the find, then retreated towards safer ground.

Their small boat was stashed in a remore spot, a quarter mile down the beach. Weather had deteriorated to the point they couldn't see anything 100 yards away. They didn't realize they were on the brink of a newly developed Gulf hurricane, without shelter.

They discovered their half-sunken skiff as tides rolled relentlessly in. Marooned on the shallow island and east of Baffin Bay, there were no towns within easy reach. One of the men was bowled over by the wind and a giant wave, scraped across a rocky shoal. His arm was deeply cut as he fell. They had to get out, fast. They struggled across the mile-wide island and the churning Laguna Madre waterway. By the time they reached a fisherman's cabin, they were relieved to have escaped with their lives.

Two days later they slogged back to find the entire coastline changed. A 30-foot high sand dune now loomed over their former campsite. Nothing of their gear remained except the half-buried, tattered frame of a folding chair. Miles of the beach had disappeared under four feet of water. Probes into the sand revealed nothing. After two full days of digging, they left; vowing to come back for their treasure. But one thing they knew; somewhere, somehow, just east of Griffin Point, the rotting remains of a Spanish galleon lay buried under the sand. And 18 Pieces-of-Eight, tied in a tight knot in the red bandana, says they will be back, no matter what.

The 110-mile sand spit is just a part of Texas' Pirate history. From Brownsville and Matamoros at the mouth of the Rio Grande, to the Buccaneer strongholds of Porto LaVaca, Galveston and Port Arthur, The Texas coast has witnessed more than its share of proud ships come to a bitter end, and covered even more treasures with shifting sands and shallow bays. For four centuries the Gulf of Mexico has used its natural currents to dump untold riches onto the beach, then changed the landmarks that pinpoint them.

There is all kinds of treasure, from Spanish gold and jewels to whiskley in kegs, ancient bottles, antique guns, as well as modern treasure such as lumber, rum, drums of oil, and every other sort of commodity carried by ship. A host of ocean-going ships of all kinds lie in the shallow bays, bayous, and inlets. Most, lying in waters less than 50-ft. deep, require few hazardous dives. Many prizes can be found walking beaches after a storm.

Hernando Cortez was only a youngster when Columbus began the European conquest of Central and South America. After vanquishing Mexico and Montezuma's tribes, his demands for riches became insatiable. The Indians brought gold, silver, and jewels to the Spanish coffers, then were pressed into slave labor to mine more in huge quantities.

Treasure laden galleons conjoined in fleets of 20 or more at Veracruz on the Mexican coast, moved to

Puerto Plata or Havana befored embarking for Spain.

In the summer months they were in grave danger of hurricanes, but apparently did not understand the time-tables of these storms. Galleons were unmanageable in wild seas. One fleet of 20 ships sailed into the teeth of a monstrous storm off the Bay of Campeche on the Yucatan Penninsula. Turning northward in a desparate attempt to avoid it, the galleons instead moved directly into its path. After two days, 16 of the treasure ships were driven onto the shoals along Padre Island's middle and destroyed. Three others disappeared and were never heard from again. The 20th ship had turned southeast, escaped the hurricane, then continued on to Spain. A priest on that boat was able to identify the location of the foundered flotilla.

A year later salvage ships arrived at Padre and began to recover the treasure. Fifteen galleons were located and most of their gold retrieved. The 16th was never found. With evidence the storm went inland, most experts assumed the missing galleons rest near the island's center point. Some speculate the galleons could have been swept across the island and foundered in the pass beyond, but the Spanish didn't press their hunt that far. However, treasure continues to turn up now and then. Once, years ago, a beachcomber prowling the island saw a small barrel sticking out of the sand. He pried it open, to discover it was packed with gold coins.

Farther up the coast, Jean LaFitte – "The Pirate of the Gulf" – supposedly buried treasure. After he was banished from New Orleans, he moved his entire fleet to Isla Serpientes (Snake Island) and changed its name to

Galveston, supposedly to impress a Mexican noble by that name, so he might count on immediate acceptance.

Later, a U.S. Navy Lieutenant Kearny, who was noted for breaking up Pirate gangs, forced LaFitte to go south, where he ended up at Isla Mujeres, at the tip of the Yucatan. Legend still holds that every cove along the Gulf Coast has its buried cache of LaFitte treasure.

In the 1500s to 1700s, Spanish Conquistadores crushed the Central and South American Indian nations and forced them into slave labor to mine silver and gold from the mountains. They smelted the ore into coins and ingots to ship, via tall, ornate and ungainly galleons, sailing across the Atlantic for Ferdinand and Isabella's growing wealth. The route became known as the Spanish Main. In summer, Spanish galleons carried tons of the coins, Dubloons, Pieces-of-Eight and other artifacts from the New World. Spain used fleeets of warships and heavily armed fortresses to protect the treasure; but they had no defense against the vicious hurricanes.

The quest for Pirate gold still runs in earnest along Florida's Atlantic Coast. Perhaps its most monstrous hurricane havoc occurred in 1715, again in summer; July 31. The Spanish Plate Fleet – for the Spanish word silver, *Plata* – 11 galleons overloaded with gold and silver on the way to Spain. The route gained a the sailing advantage, Gulf Stream's northern current, which curves up the coast and then eastward. It could take weeks off the voyage, assuming all things went well.

However, that was not to be their destiny, as the horrendous storm drove the hapless galleons to the sand and rocks. A Queen's dowry of inestimable wealth aboard, faltered at midnight as the storm struck. 11 ships spewed their treasures along a 25 mile path. Pirates skull and cross-bones, weren't involved. When salvage operations began, local Indian tribes – Timacuans – helped those who survived. More than 700 people were lost.

Today at the McLarty Museum in Melbourne Beach, FL, a monumental Indian Mound, 75' high, celebrates the event, and the tribes which helped, although there are no known descendents of either. The museum, located where the survivors built a campsite while waiting for rescue, has many coins and artifacts dating from that time.

Now, when a hurricane sweeps the Florida coast, seas rocketing with merciless power; the next days host the faithful; hopeful treasure hunters. Some wielding expensive metal detecting equipment, others simply raking the sand, trusting to luck.

The State Park doesn't allow vistors to keep any objects found on its land.

Our own metal detecting expedition at Padre Island, as we stated earlier, instead followed almost the same path as the first pair of treasure hunters we described. Except that we weren't lucky enough to come upon the 18 gold dubloons. When we finally got back, and dug down to the material that made our hearts dance, and our metal detectors chime like organs, it wasn't silver or gold. Unfortunately, is was a bent, rusted bicycle which had apparently been lost some years before. It had waited patiently to be a part of our Pirate Treasure tale. So it was -- an almost treasure.

Yet we are still convinced, it's down there, somewhere close. Just waiting to be found.

Perhaps next time...

#

CAPT. CHUCK GNAEGY

Sixteen

Pirates in Caribbean History

It Don't Mean a Thing if You Ain't Got that Ding-a-ling

For all cruisers of the sea, the now famous farewell chant by the most notorious Pirate bears repeating here: For all who admire Pirates of the Caribbean, there's a message to remember:

"My name was Captain Kidd, when I sail'd, when I sail'd, And so wickedly I did, God's laws I did forbid, When I sail'd, when I sail'd. I roam'd from sound to sound, And many a ship I found, And then I sunk or burn'd, When I sail'd. I murder'd William Moore, And laid him in his gore, Not many leagues from shore, When I sail'd. Farewell to young and old, All jolly seamen bold, You're welcome to my gold, For I must die, I must die. Farewell to Lunnon town, The pretty girls all round, No pardon can be found, and I must die, I must die; Farewell, for I must die. Then to eternity, in hideous misery, I must lie, I must lie."

Part Two: Ru*m* Away, Paradise Down Island

Cruising and Live-Aboards

Georgetown, Exuma, St. Thomas, St. John, USVI, St. Lucia, are havens for liveaboards, the lucky few who ran away to sea, and made it work. All kinds are there, from your 72 foot Hatteras to a little 29 foot California one bedroom efficiency sloop. Everything in between. The 125+s are there too, but in a different location, not mingling with the riff-rafts. Anchor out there and join 50 to a hundred or more any time of the year, but particularly the winter months. For hurricane season some boats, especially the charters, move to Trinidad in the deep Caribbean. Georgetown is a delightful anchorage.

Cruisers I've met there:
There is Arnold Murphy, who doesn't want to sail around the world, just get away. Sick of mowing lawns and fighting traffic morning and night, he ached to live somewhere close to the ocean, but to keep on teaching. The last year he worked in Chicago he drove 29,000 miles in a year, just going to work. Now he does not own a car but a 36 foot sloop. He goes back every summer to Ft. Lauderdale, teaches summer school.

Then there is my good friend Captain Kernblower. He guided his 48 foot trawler to Georgetown and did not want to leave, except for maybe a three month jaunt to Venezuela, stopping at every island in the Windward chain of jewels along the way. With his white beard, battered sneakers, and cut-offs, he looks just like Sean Connery; you would not know he is a retired airline captain. His influence is strong in this book, in several wild stories. Now he does whatever he wants. That is, he wants to dive for lobsters, do a little fishing, creep around the million little cays and wonderful, deserted beaches. "The sand here," he croaks, "is spun sugar, whiter than snow."

Bob and Jennie built their own boat, a catamaran 32 feet long, from plans they found in a boating magazine by Charles Kanter. Took them three years of part time labor, but didn't cost much, except for the engines – two Yanmar diesels nestled inside the hulls. They do all the work together. If their boat needs a repair, they know how to do it. "It's like living in a little trailer," Jennie says, "but you get used to it. I like it better than some apartments we've had." She makes pottery to sell.

Sure, there are all kinds down island. Two boats last year stopped just for a while, on their way around the world. Last time I heard from them they were in Tahiti. Caught in a typhoon, their boat was up on "the hard," having a bit of replacement surgery. An industrial engineer specializing in city power and light facilities, he has the skills to take an interim job anywhere in the world. They are not coming back here until they complete their merry-go-round. Who would?

So how do you make a living? Bill and Barbara

Larrabie charter their 45 foot *Yellow Bird* for over $1000 a week, per couple, four months during the season, as captain and crew/cook. They have the rest of the year to themselves, living well. They say even the chartering is fun. "I do not know how I put up with the life I led before," Bill says. "Life on the water, down here, is something very different, satisfying, a strange new world."

If you really want to do this, you'll find a way.

The Down Island Voyage Continues:

Richard Argh-Argh and I took a couple of days to make *MoonDancer* all right again, as possible. I dove down and chopped the melted nylon rope off the prop. No apparent damage, no leaks, no wobbling. The engine was cleared to operate.

A tedious job was stitching up the rips in the main. That entailed patch kits, sail tape, strong nylon thread, awl, and a bosun's palm with a needle the size of a ballpoint pen filler. But soon it was as shipshape as we could get it. An old wood boat, it would never be brand new again. Hours were spent to sort out and restore the trifles and treasures, the junk, back to their cubbyholes and lockers in the cabins. Generator was no worse for the dunking.

Too bad the head did not swim overboard and rid us forever of that redolent stink. Richard, when he first got this boat, made an ingenious loop in the air intake. He was unsure if it would be safe to vent the evacuation line up above the cabin, so he inset a valve that lets the gases escape *into* the head compartment. A very bright coup, and safe, he thinks. But the monumental stench is the total Brooklyn Zoo head evacuation station.

No one, except him, wants to be anywhere near that head. I fear his entire olfactory mechanism must be brain dead. I prefer a wooden bucket, in the open cockpit if necessary. Primitive means on a primitive sailboat. Anchored out down island, he sees no reason for saving the goop and patronizing a pumping station, if there would happen to be one. He avoids areas that require those rules. However, the rest of us are still saddled with the ungodly odors of his collective BMs. That goes double when we are sleeping and he is up carousing all night. We need to lock him in there for a week, and try for a forced cure.

But, it is his boat. He does it his way. Hooray.

We started out again for Calabash Bay. Is this where old-style comic Jimmy Durante's mamu was born and raised? "Goodnight, Mrs. Calabash," he always said, signing off. But it is simply a nice little semi-circular cove at the north end of Long Island, protected from the prevailing southeasterly breeze. Halfway there, the weather started to throw us another curve ball.

Clouds were forming in the eastern quadrant, those dimply, threatening tornadic formations that drop funnels down on Kansas and the Everglades, and suck up whole blocks of houses, or the deer and the antelope that play in its way.

But at sea, those funnels become Water Spouts. Perhaps not quite as powerful or destructive as land-based tornadoes, they wreak havoc on any small boat that may stumble into its path. Tales are rife about ruined superstructure, destroyed deckhouses, blown out window ports, ripped off sails, and in some very rare cases, loss of lives. Dangerous anomalies lurk in Mother nature's quiver.

"I see it," Richard said when I pointed it out. "Nothing we can do. Don't know which way it might turn. Hold your course." He went below for his afternoon nap, boning up zees for the night in port, when he will want to carouse until three ayem.

The spiral funnel cloud was a long way off, perhaps fifteen miles, and at our five or six knots, it could be gone long before we arrive under its snaky finger.

Then as I watched , monitoring its course, it dipped down first one, then another, slender, round tentacle, probing for the ocean's surface. The first digit reached all the way, thousands of feet, and even from this distance I could see a spurting asterisk of foam and waves where the finger jabbed, glinting, reflecting the slanting sunlight.

Sparkling, goosing a great wiggle in the water. Who could be on the other end of that finger?

It traced that course perhaps a mile, then broke its contact, gradually shortening the finger, until at last it was absorbed again by the dimpled cloud. The second finger just hung there, tapered to a very slender point, just peering at the sea, not venturing downward. At least it didn't turn up. It waved around like an elephant's trunk searching for a stray apple, then gave up, shortening gradually until it was back in the fold. I was glad we were not there.

I watched this probing several times in the next hour

and a half as we approached our anchoring point at Calabash. If it hung around another hour, I did not want to venture in and get sucked up in the maelstrom. Dick was snoring like a garbage truck down below, so I had the tiller to myself.

And gradually, I saw the clouds retract. The afternoon was calming, heat was dissipating, fewer extreme pressures were there to modulate a difference in cloud formations.

We were a mile from our anchorage point, when again I gazed skyward. Straight up, into the most perfect galactic formation I've ever seen. A perfect spiral of cloud work perhaps twenty miles across, slender white tentacles coiled in a concentric whirl against deep blue sky, spiraling to the center where a large cobalt dot pulsed dark to light, light to dark. Nothing short of amazing. A glimpse into a sliced-open nautilus shell high in the sky, perhaps ten miles across. A phenomenon.

E.T.? Is that you? Was this cut-in-half cephalopod shell a heavenly mollusk phenomenon or a space ship seed pod? Or was it the nucleus of a water spout that was forming to suck the life, us that is, out of this wallowing old she-goat sailboat? Why was each white tentacle so symmetrically coiled, perfectly tapered and aligned? Any one of them could be the next finger that writes its sparkle on the wall of the ocean.

I stared at it for long minutes as we traversed directly underneath the center. I felt a chill run up my backbone, waiting for it to show its hand, its finger to do its deed. If it was going to descend upon us, now was the time. I was the only one in the world who knew this spaceship was there. Would it flash down and kidnap me, so I could someday be on David Letterman's *Dumb Boat Tricks* and tell my story to a hooting audience of Noo Yawk scholars and rednecks? I contemplated this strange emergence and wondered what it meant, if anything. But it did not develop; faded, gradually.

"Argh Argh! We are almost in Calabash," Richard said, breaking my reverie, climbing up from below. "Take a course for that lone tree on top the ridge and we'll anchor about seventy-five yards off shore. It is good holding ground. We'll spend the night there." He glanced at my face, moved in close to peer up at me.

"Are you okay? You're pale. You are not sick, or praying, are you? I don't think you pray. You believe in something up there?"

"Yeah," I said. "I believe, for a moment, I saw right into the eye of the universe, just for a split second."

"And what did it tell you?"

"It said, where in the Grand Cosmos did I hide that rum bottle?"

"I hear you," he answered. "You know, when I first came to the Carry-Bee-hind I was a scotch drinker. Good scotch. Teacher's. Single malts. But when I found out scotch was thirty-five dollars a bottle, and rum was two dollars, it was an easy choice to make."

"Roger that," I said. "Did you know that spiral galaxies and water sprouts can sometimes cause hallucinations in susceptible, even sober, sailors?"

"Argh, argh. I think you must be shipping out too heavy, you are into deep analysis." He lumbered forward to the bow, choosing a sheltered spot that looked to be out of the wind sheer off the nearby eminence of Bahama's Long Island, at Calabash Bay. Clean water. We were alone.

"We'll anchor here. Round up and drop the main."

"Aye, aye, captain." Glancing upward, I did not see any trace of my sliced-down-the-middle partitioned-chambered nautilus any more, up in the sky. My figment had escaped. My spiritual connection, if there was one, like they say on the internet, was now disconnected. I did not have skymail from up above. The entire episode was unidentified, unharmed, unnamed.

Unreal.

We anchored. Captain Dick came ambling to the bow, where I set the anchor and cleated down the hawser. We set another, shorter anchor and rode from the bow, at 180 degrees from the first. That is a "Bahama Rig" so the boat does not swing around in the night in case of a wind shift. It's very useful in case other boats are anchored in the same place.

That evening, however, for a while it looked like we were the sole inhabitants of Calabash Bay. But he had noticed something while I was distracted with the anchoring. Another sailboat motored in slowly, less than a hundred yards off our stern, and stopped, wallowed, looking for a good spot.

This is always the case. Find a nice quiet, lonely anchorage and the next guy who comes wants to drop his anchor right next door, right in your lap, sometimes 10 yards away, with his boombox blaring. We had five miles on any side, and all good water, yet this never-fail visitor slipped in, a softball pitch away. So much for solitude. We attract visitors like flies on honey, or dog doo-doo, take your pick.

But Richard was excited about this one. "That boat! I know her, she is *Music Maven*! I'd know her anywhere!" He waved. "Hey! Ahoy Music Maven! It is I, Captain Dick. Dick Moore! Hey! I know you!"

He rushed down below, emerged from the cabin with a battered bugle in his hand. He blew it madly, honking some insane yodel. Not music, but a horny blast any she-goat would turn flips for.

The skipper of the other boat climbed slowly out from the cockpit, and weaving unsteadily, like a giant sloth, reached the foredeck. Weaving? This was calm water. What? It was a woman! She grabbed tight on the forestay with both hands. Squinted her eyes.

"R-ii-ich-ch, Aaaaard?" she called.

"Argghh!" I knew it! "Hey! ArghArghArgh! It is I. It is Richard!"

"Whhooppeeee!" She cried. "What a nice soup-prize! I am so happy! I want to see you, Riiichch-aaard!" She waved both hands, suddenly lost her footing and stumbled against the bow pulpit. Caught herself. "I have not see-een you for soooo long, Riiichch-aaard."

He turned to me. "I've got to launch the dinghy! I've got to go see her. This is Melodie Mayo, my long lost love, out of the Miami Philharmonic Orchestra. Help me get this dinghy in the water!" I thought he had toys in his attic.

"But your dinghy's an inflatable," I said. "We have

to think about blowing it up first."

"Oh. Yeah," he said, "Argh-Argh," suddenly chastened, suddenly aware we were not sitting in Key Largo at the dock.

"Tell her it'll be a few minutes. Is she here by herself? A woman single-handing?"

"I better ask her." He went to holler. "Hey, Melodie, are you single handing?"

She sank down on the foredeck, barely hanging on to the stanchion. "Ye-e-es. Wheeen caaan yoou gheeet here? Cooome over for driiinks an' dinnnn-er. Cooome in an hour." She lolled, swayed against the stanchion.

"Hey, Richard," I said, "I do not think she is going to be ready for din-din in an hour. I think she'll pass out right there, and we'll have to wipe her up off the deck and put her to bed."

He didn't listen to me. Instead, he shouted, "Melodie, my love, we will be there in one hour! I have my crew with me. We will be there!" He turned to me. "Get that dinghy out from the lazarette, and we'll blow her up." He rubbed his hands in glee.

"My Melodie. She got her name because her daddy was a champion barber shop quartet singer; she was conceived on the night of his climax, er, greatest triumph. Melodeeeee. I have such good luck I cannot stand it!"

Within the hour we prepared the dinghy, and ourselves, for din-din as the guest of the Miami Philharmonic maven. I still had questions – was she alone? If so, how did she get here? We did not see her in Georgetown. Where did she come from?

We rowed the few yards to her boat and tapped on the hull. She staggered up from below into the cockpit. She was wearing — a dress. Pretty bangles in her wild red hair. The smell of spaghetti sauce emanated from the cabin, along with something else, barely unidentifiable. Richard introduced me to "The love of my life. Melodie Mayo."

A snowflake. She was not a bad looker, but I could tell she was a victim of alcohol abuse, to say the least. The Carry-bee-hind sailing disease. Slightly bloated cheeks, puffy, hazy eyes. A soft grey smile. By herself, having left her companion at Stella Maris after a round house disagreement. But she was no jiffy pop, she maintained, a capable sailor, able to handle her boat anywhere in any condition. I was gratified to hear that, since she was still in no condition to be sailing anywhere.

She broke out a bottle of Chilean wine, Concha y Toro, red, and uncorked it. Poured each of us a half pint genuine stemware glass full. I tasted it, rolled it around my palate. Veddy good. As good as I have drunk in Margarita, Venezuela, and yes, I can still remember that. Richard tipped his glass up and drained it dry, gulp, gulp, gulp. "Ahhhhhhh! That is good wine!" He was perfectly in his element.

"I hope you like spaghetti," she offered. "It is the easiest thing to make. And I am out of steaks for the time being." She was fluttering about like Martha Stewart hosting the governors' ball. I suspected she also had been toying with the rum bottle before and after we arrived.

Turned out she had been a member of the Miami

Philharmonic Orchestra, one of the organizers, she said, and loved music over anything in the world. Except her cats, of which four are on this boat right now, and of which one is rubbing itself into heat on my calf. I am not a cat person, but I did not wish to offend her either. I confess I smelled the cat boxes long before we even entered the boat. They are like smokers; they can run but they cannot hide their stink. Even downwind, cat odor spreads itself over the open ocean like invisible fog, impossible to avoid. But that is not all. Whether she was also without her cleaning lady, was also too obvious. And I saw, slowly crawling up the wall next to my arm, a middle-size Carry-bee-hind cockroach. One, then two, another, if not many. That was not the restaurant of which I would choose to become a permanent patron.

I was trapped. Richard was having the time of his life with Melodie Mayonnaise. We ate the spaghetti, drank the wine, and afterward retired to the main cabin, gabbing, telling lies. I learned her life was spent with music, arranging it, organizing it, promoting it. And gradually I received the vibes that told me this is not a potential menage a trois, if it ever was; and to leave them alone, to their wine, their rum, their cigarettes, their discovery of each other, their feline aromas, and/or whatever may perhaps come next.

I was very glad to excuse myself and head for the dinghy. I assumed Richard would trumpet me when, and if, he decided to return.

I dozed in the salon, expecting Richard would signal me somehow. But eventually I saw it was four ayem,

I headed for my bunk, thankful that my captain would not be using the head this early.

I heard them, at last, rowing noisily in her dinghy, carousing, ringing little finger bells, chirping operatic phrases, love songs, to each other, banging the dinghy against the hull. But I was too exhausted to complain. I knew when she gave up to go home, it was cranking up daylight; it was a night he'd remember for a long time.

I thought she'd go back to Stella Maris, back to her other musical muse, whomever that may be.

The next morning dawned bright and sunny, but the winds were eighteen and up, southeast as usual. We did not feel it, in our cozy cove. I weighed anchor and raised the main, hoisted the jib, and started the engine. Waved bye bye to philharmonic Melodie Mayonaise. We were going to round Long Island's little bluff at Cape Santa Maria, and head over to Rum Cay. How appropo for my captain, who was still in the sack sleeping off that entire jug of wine and liter of rum that lulled him to sleep last night at dawn.

It was a short hop to Rum Cay, a little potato chip island surrounded by rocky reefs. I did not know the way in, but Richard, now awake, instructed me:

"I know this like the back of my hand." This was enough to warn me; beware of Arrgghs bearing wise counsel. Shallow water, big rocks just underneath. Still a quarter mile offshore when there was a sudden sickening crunch; our bow lifted up about a foot, and *MoonDancer* was halted in midrise.

"Back her down!" he ordered.

I shifted into reverse and teased the engine. Didn't

budge. Didn't even shudder.

"Harder!" Richard shouted. I did. It didn't.

"We are hard aground, or arock," I said. Our bow is poking up at blue Hawaii."

"Okay. Get your mask on. See what is down there."

I did that. In seconds I was under the boat. We were in barely five and a half feet, with our four and a half foot draft. But the culprit was a big, hard, V-shaped rock that snuggled under our keel. I swam over to it. Perhaps, with a little coaxing, we'd get off. I bent down to get a closer look. There, next to the rock, was a small wooden barrel, a beer keg. Stuffed inside that keg was a million spiny lobsters. Well, maybe 50 or 75. A whole family. At least 60, if my eyes did not lie to me. I was completely sober, why would they?

I backed off slowly, popped to the top, and delivered my news. Richard did not care that much. "Argh Argh," he groans, " Who can think about eating lobsters when we are stuck on some rock that was not there the last time?"

"I can," I retort. "And it is almost lunch time."

"Never mind them. Get me off! Arrggh!"

"First things first," I said, digging in my heels. "I love lobster, and this is the mother lode. Hand me a big board, or a net, or your pillow. I am going to stop up the top of that keg, and drag them up."

He rummaged in the hatch. Came out with …nothing. "I got nothing," he says, not willing to cooperate.

"Damn it, Richard, just give me my bath towel then. And some rope. I will take care of them in no time."

I took the towel and line and slipped forward. The beasts were milling in and out, a million spiny arms and legs and antennae feelers piled up in a clump inside that wooden keg. A Lobster Legion Convention.

I slapped the towel over the end, took a couple of turns around it with the line, and they were mine. Heavy, though. I wrestled the ungainly prize to the stern, tied a couple more loops top and bottom, and handed it up. Richard had the main halyard to clip on it, then winched it up.

"Okay, now. We got your lobsters. Get my boat loose!"

"Aye, sir," I saluted. "Start your engine, and when I am in front to heave, sock it in reverse. I'll put my shoulder in it."

The first two times it did not budge. Third try, I felt a little gritty movement. I heaved, putting my whole back into it and shoving with my knees. It backed off. Free. At last.

I stood up on the rock to see what was happening. Suddenly the boat was boiling backward in a big circle, full bore, and Richard was jumping in and out of the cockpit, doing a crazed highland fling. "They are loose!" he shouted. "Wild animals. Giant spiders! All over my deck! They tried to crawl up my shorts!"

"Stop the engine!" I shouted back. "You are circling back to the same rock quarry, stern first! Slap it in neutral. Quick!"

In quicktime, he got it done. She stopped within three feet of the rock, and me, propeller first. I was in the cowardly act of scrunching down into the water to escape the prop when, looking up through the roiled water, I saw my herd of lobsters falling, one by one, off the side.

I spluttered to the top. "What are you doing with my lobsters? These animals are worth ten dollars apiece."

He was sweeping them out, one at a time, with a broom.

"ArghArghArgh -- they piss me off, scooting around like that, backwards. Stabbing me with their chopsticks! They attacked me! Crawling up my cut-offs."

I swam to the boat and grappled myself back in. Fewer than a dozen were left.

"Damn it Dick. What the hell are you doing?"

"Aa -rr-gg-hh! I do not eat lobster," he growled. "They are big bugs."

"Well I do, and if you throw any more of these overboard, you won't be eating any solid food for a couple of weeks!"

"ARGArghArghArghARgh!"

That was the end of Rum Cay, the lobsters, and our conversation for the next whole day. He pouted. I pouted. We were stuck together on this boat and not speaking to each other. These are grown men?

But our adventure was not over.

By late afternoon, next day, we sighted the strange boiling eruption that marks Hell Gate, at Crooked and Acklins Island, Land Rail Point, Lovely Bay, and deserted crescent Atwood Harbor. We were speaking to each other again – was this like a marriage, or what? – and he was on the bow, guiding me in with hand motions to a good anchorage. It was routine. We droppd the hook, broke out the rum, and lounged on the fantail. After a hard day's sail I was hot and sweaty. I decided to take a "Joy shower."

That is a bucket of seawater dipped from over the side, a sponge, and a bottle of Joy liquid, the best thing we've ever found to lather in salt water. Dip in the sponge, squirt the Joy, and rub it down. Smells good, lathers better. Then leap into the sea to clean it off. Whooeee-mama!

Except, as I finished lathering and was ready for the plunge, I glanced down into the clear bay – always a good idea to look before you leap, here.

"Hey, Captain Chuck," Richard said. "Argh. Do not jump in yet. Take a bow. You have got an audience about to applaud your entrance."

What did I see, gazing back at me with cold, yellow eyes measuring my girth, anticipating my entry? A toothy bull shark at least ten feet long, an arm's length off the stern. That was a full-sized 55-gallon drum with teeth. I thought perhaps I'd just dump the bucket over my head; I had second thoughts about plunging in. And third thoughts.

I thought of a friend in Key Largo who worked for one year to build his boat for the great down-island adventure – cruise and booze, live off the fish in the sea, not a care in the universe. He sailed as far as Hole in the Wall, at Abaco, and after sailing all day, hot and sweaty, did the Joy shower thing, just like I was about to do.

But when he dove in, it was apparently right into the jaws of Jaws, which removed a large chunk out of his thigh. It was touch and go. BASRA, Bahama Air Sea Rescue got him to Nassau Victoria Hospital; one pint of blood still pumping, but a very close call. He was in recovery for a long time.

From there south by east are the Plana Cays, where we saw the finest virgin reefs ever, absolute hordes of fish, all types, crowding into steeples of coral, long corridors packed with porkfish, mackerel, angelfish, jacks, tuna, yellowtail, all milling, mingling, barely missing each other as they teemed like the five o'clock rush on Noo Yawk's Fifth Avenue.

Shoot a spear down this carnival hallway, and you'd bag a dozen varieties with one arrow. William Tell would get a hundred. We had no ice, and no working fridge, so it would be no use to spear this easy game. We let them go. My pleasure was to swim in there, and feel them bump me, nudge me, then back off, and go around. It was, truly, a piscatawary jungle down there.

But soon we were at the mysterious Mayaguana Island, not a general stop for cruisers, but a must for me. Picking our way into the wide Abraham Bay through glowering coral palisades into a turquoise blue expanse, half a mile by a couple of miles. The settlement is small and very rustic. One cramped general store and bar.

But in half a mile was a 10,000 foot airstrip. It was built by the U.S. Air Force when we invaded the Dominican Republic in the 1960s, to scare off the commies with U.S. Marines. The airstrip then had service from BahamasAir twice a week. I wanted to buy a ticket to Noo Yawk, to attend a very special wedding, within two days. I would leave Richard the Monte Cristo here to find another crew for the D/R. I would not make it to my isle of Eden in the raw, not this time, but there will be others.

This trip had taken longer than we planned, and now I had to go.

Friday dawned and I bid goodbye to Cap'n Argh Dick. It was a ball that ended, too soon. When I arrived at the airport I met a local policeman from Nassau. I wondered why he might be there, a long way from his bailiwick. Was something going on with this out of the way island that we should not know about? Perhaps that nice long airstrip was being utilized by someone for something other than the once-a-week ex-cape flights?

The cop said, "no available seats on this plane." "I have to get a seat," I said. "I'll pay anyone a hundred dollars for their seat, plus the ticket."

The crowd swelled, local mamas and papas, curly haired pequeno ninos in bright dresses lined up for the airplane. When they began to load, the stewardess trundled down the stairs, picked me out from the crowd. "You. Yellah hair! You ain't goin'." I was the only yellow hair in a thousand miles.

"But, I've got to go!" I said. "I'll pay anyone one hundred dollars for their seat, plus my seventy-five dollar ticket! Anyone? Please?" I waved a wad of 20s. I was desperate. "Hundred and fifty!" It was all I had.

" Anyone? Please! Please!"

Next plane was a week away; I would miss my wonderful daughter's wedding. I couldn't face that.

They left me standing on the tarmac as the big twin

engine plane roared off down the runway. I was devastated. My Bahamian Caribbean Odyssey had turned to horse glue in my mouth. I sagged there on the blacktop.

Killed.

Does a grown man fall to his knees and bawl like a child who has missed Christmas; the most important event in his life? I confess.

"Hey, Key Largo," a voice said from behind. I turned, and it was the Nassau cop. "Dere is a plane you can get," he says.

"Where? I'll take it!"

"De governuh's plane, a Piper Aztec, comes in today with the Nassau Drug Commissionuh. He stays overnight, but de plane go back today. You can get on it. I take you dere."

I was almost blubbering. This sort of luck never happens to me. A savior was in my midst. He ushered me to the back of a hangar; on the tarmac was a beautiful, twin-engine Piper Aztec. He talked with the pilot, who motioned me to get on with my bag.

I thanked my benefactor profusely. I did not know how to thank him. If I kissed his hand, he'd probably smack me. I did not want to know, or ask, why the Nassau Drug Commissioner would be visiting this sparsely populated, remote out island. That was another whole story I might look into perhaps later. I did not want to know anything about this flight except that I was a passenger.

I climbed aboard. The pilot grinned at me. "That is one hundred twenty-five dolluhs, please." He held out his hand. I did not ask how he added up the price.

I was glad to pay. I rode shotgun all the way back, right seat, up front, gazing rapturously out the windshield at the marvelous, striking beauty of Bahamian/Caribbean waters and sky. It was indeed a visual paradise down there. Why does anyone live in NooYawk?

At Nassau, I checked through Customs and boarded a plane for Big Apple City. I was a happy man. I had gone down to the sea in ships, and lived to tell this tale.

This fine and noble adventure had come to an end. It was over. I entertained no regrets. There will be many others to come.

I 'll be Back

#

PIRATES, PEARLS & PARADISE

CAPT. CHUCK GNAEGY

PIRATES, PEARLS & PARADISE